Au Paris

Au Paris

A Memoir

RACHEL SPENCER

CITADEL PRESS
Kensington Publishing Corp.
www.kensingtonbooks.com

CITADEL PRESS BOOKS are published by

Kensington Publishing Corp.
850 Third Avenue
New York, NY 10022

Copyright © 2006 Rachel Spencer

All Kensington titles, imprints, and distributed lines are available at special quantity discounts for bulk purchases for sales promotions, premiums, fund-raising, educational, or institutional use. Special book excerpts or customized printings can also be created to fit specific needs. For details, write or phone the office of the Kensington special sales manager: Kensington Publishing Corp., 850 Third Avenue, New York, NY 10022, attn: Special Sales Department: phone 1-800-221-2647.

CITADEL PRESS and the Citadel logo are Reg. U.S. Pat. & TM Off.

First printing: December 2006

10 9 8 7 6 5 4 3 2

Printed in the United States of America

Library of Congress Control Number: 2006929667

ISBN 0-8065-2797-8

for Betty Claire Jackson Spencer Sample,
a storyteller whose best story was her own

Chapitre Un

It was 2 a.m. and I lay wide awake, counting the days and hours until my plane left for Paris. Three days and sixteen hours, to be exact—which I could determine neither good nor bad at that moment. This could have been for a number of reasons, really. I was high on double lattes as usual, ode to Starbucks, but I wasn't reacting with the normal incessant tapping and fidgeting. In fact, I wasn't moving at all. I felt paralyzed, emotionless to the core. Tick, tick, tick was all my mind could hear, counting the clocks in my head as if an internal bomb were about to implode me.

Months ago, I had woken up at age twenty-three to realize I was living a life I'd never planned—one I'd never even wanted. Everything I knew was wrong—who I thought was, where I thought I'd go, what I thought I'd do. All those dreams I'd had as a little girl, the pining and praying and wishing and hoping, had faded from slightly recognizable to non-existent sometime during and after college. I didn't know what to feel or what to do. So I changed it all. In a matter of one week, I stripped myself of a job, an apartment, a community, and any familiar environment in an effort to regain what I had lost. Though at that time, I wasn't sure what lost was.

Paris was the fresh start, the place to begin the search for the life I had been missing. But, not being independently wealthy, I had to find a way to travel there without breaking the bank. I had heard about au pair programs—my sister had actually lived in Paris as an au pair for one year. I visited her there, met the family, stayed in their house. We had a great time. It seemed an easy enough set-up, with maximum reward for minimal effort, so I explored the option for myself. As luck would have it, they needed a summer nanny, they being the Vladescos—*les Vladesco*—Alex and Estelle, whose three children, Diane, 14, Léonie, 11, and Constantin, 7, I agreed to keep for six weeks while I lived in their home. An au pair in Paris—it was a good place to start.

Les Vladesco lived right in the *centre ville,* just near the l'Arc de Triomphe, which meant that a daily walk on the Champs, kids in tow, would become part of my regular routine. The whole thing sounded foreign to me, no pun intended, considering I had spent the past two and a half years reporting to a cubicle every weekday morning. The anxiety from quitting my job had only begun taking its toll when, two weeks after my last day in the office, nothing was direct deposited into my checking. True, losing one's source of income can rattle the most sound-minded of folks, but crazier still—I'd done it voluntarily.

For nearly three years, I worked in ad sales for the *Houston Chronicle*. It was what most people would call a good job.

Good company. Great people. Fun industry. Looking back, now that I was unemployed, I had to mention the additional perk of health insurance. (Though I'd heard that if I should require medical assistance during my summer abroad, the one good thing about French government was free doctor visits.)

Perks aside, I wasn't inspired. Sure, I liked certain things about the *Chronicle* job. I even *loved* certain things about it—especially dressing the part, which was the easiest way to mask a deep-rooted dissatisfaction with my life in general. On my best days, I would avoid the truth in my never-fail black power suit from J. Crew: a dashing wool gabardine duo combining the four-button blazer and pencil skirt with daring back slit. And the shoes were twice as important. How I relied upon my darling and oh-so-sleek black Stuart Weitzman stilettos, so much so that my closest co-worker referenced them in her goodbye note to me: "Wherever life takes you, may you always walk with Stuies on your feet," she wrote. She was the one who inducted me into the Stuart Weitzman club, you see, and into all the other couture clubs beyond. Before her, I didn't even know how to pronounce Louis Vuitton.

But the rest of the time—as in the actual eight hours a day I was paid to work and not just prance the streets of downtown, albeit under the façade of a great wardrobe—I felt like a prisoner in my own cubicle. One afternoon as I sat watching the minutes on my computer screen clock change from one to the next, it occurred to me there could be more satisfying life quests. I was in need of drastic change. So I started plotting my escape plan right there from my jail cell of a cubicle.

I figured to really walk away, I needed a clean start,

back to the basics, back to school. I wanted to be a writer. So what was I doing in advertising? I had deceived myself into believing if I took the advertising job at a newspaper, I could segue into editorial. Nothing was further from the truth. I was building a great resume for a sales career, but writing had nothing to do with it. It was time to change that. So I decided to go back to school to pursue my master's in journalism.

I spent countless hours at my desk with open Word documents typing a statement of interest and cover letters to those from whom I would request recommendations. I typed my application. I took a vacation day to take the GRE. In the space of the test designated to mark which schools should receive the scores, I entered the University of Arkansas, Fayetteville, where I'd gone to undergraduate school. Columbia would have been nice, but New York sounded scary. I'm sure there were plenty of other choices, but Fayetteville sounded easy, even comforting after years of slaving in an unrewarding job. I knew people there. I would be taken care of there. So I decided to make a new beginning by going back to where I started. At the time, I was so sure it was the right decision that I rented an apartment there before I was even accepted into school. I had that remarkable impetuous quality.

But before the next phase of my life—before I moved back to Fayetteville, Arkansas, for grad school (even though I didn't know yet whether I was accepted)—I needed a serious vacation. Since I wasn't too far out of college, I still remembered the three months of bliss that were summer vacation. I wanted them. After being a cubicle dweller in a job I didn't like, I'd earned them. Besides, because I was starting grad school in the fall (if I got in), I was practically a student already. So I planned my vacation—the pre-grad school last hurrah, so to speak. I wanted it to be good, something I'd remember forever.

I sent an e-mail to my sister with the subject: "Do the Vladescos need an au pair this summer?" Sarah has always taken care of me and I usually expect her to know everything. In fact, she usually does. So I wasn't surprised when, not too many days later, an email arrived in my inbox from Estelle Vladesco. "Summer Au Pair Position" was the subject. We discussed arrival and departure dates and, knowing I'd been before and we'd already met, there was an instantaneous agreement. She wanted me there by June 17; I would turn in my resignation in May. It was a bold move. But the more I thought toward making this extreme life change, the less a paycheck mattered. After all, besides Stuie and Louis, who were the true sweethearts in my life, it wasn't about the money. There was more, and I wanted to find it. And I knew it wouldn't happen by watching time tick past in my tiny cube in Houston, Texas. So I quit.

I gave a responsible thirty-day resignation notice backed by a responsible purpose: graduate studies. No corporation would ever frown on higher education for their employees. I was applauded—I was praised. How smart. How courageous. Way to go for what you really want! I leaned on the hope of a new life. Grad school would take me back to the person I was supposed to be, lead me to the career I was supposed to have, give me the life I was supposed to live. But first, a reward. First, I would spend a summer in Paris.

Rachel Spencer

After bittersweet good-byes at the *Chronicle*, I lapsed almost immediately from suit-and-stiletto mode back into the jeans and flip-flops that were my college uniform. The transition was surprisingly simple, though I'd upgraded a little since college from brown leather reefs to gold leather Capri thongs.

They're shoes, not underwear.

Having paired the sandals with trendy jeans and my green cashmere cardigan, I'd found my outfit for the plane ride and felt confident enough to cross "dress the part" off my to-do list. And that's quite an accomplishment, considering I'd made it a personal trend to equate dressing the part with success on the job. I could have spent more time brushing up on my French or reading some books on childcare, but nine hours on a plane would be time enough for that. I packed my other outfits, not quite as strategically planned as the one for the plane, in a suitcase Sarah bought for me. I stuffed in every pocket miscellaneous toiletries that seemed imperative to keep on hand in a foreign country, though I didn't use them here. Powders and gels and sprays and lotions—whether superfluous or frivolous, they all went into my suitcase. It was the biggest suitcase Samsonite made, but I had to sit on it to zip it closed. So I sat and I zipped and I set it in the hall by the front door. Before I could stare at it long enough to doubt myself, it was time to go to the airport.

"Paris is always a good idea," Julia Ormond says in *Sabrina*. When you're craving a total life makeover, it is very easy to be so persuaded by this Hollywood philosophy that the 1700 dollars it takes to fly to Paris in June seems a nominal fee. Booking the plane ticket was where the real bravery began. I damn near burst the walls of my cubicle the day I booked that ticket. Immediately there was born in me a new hope, a thrilling urgency. I imagined myself boarding the plane and a shot of that airport vibe ran through me. You know that vibe. People going places; everyone is either coming or going or starting out or ending up and no matter the occasion, there is urgency in the air. I was ready to go places and I had a ticket. I knew nannying for three kids was not exactly as glamorous as Sabrina working at *Vogue*. But it *was* a new start, and one that would *pay me* to live in Paris. Yes, Paris was a good idea indeed.

How ironic, then, that upon arriving weeks later at the airport, on the day of my departure, the thrilling urgency I'd craved, that airport vibe, felt more like sheer panic. Standing in the George Bush Intercontinental Airport of Houston *sans* job and apartment, the only urgency rising in me was the one to flee that airport, run to my parents' house, and bury myself in a hole. I surveyed the crowd. Migrating toward the gate, a huge group of travelers chattered excitedly, all high on airport fever. From the looks of their baseball hats, matching T-shirts, and fanny packs, they were probably about to embark on one of those all-inclusive, ten countries in five days, tour-guided vacation deals. Gross. They should be required by airport security or foreign immigration officers to bear signs reading BEWARE OF AMERICANS ON VACATION. Though I couldn't imagine *fanny pack* translating into any other language.

Regardless of wardrobe, the traveling herds looked excited, in love, entertained, or at least accompanied. I, on the other hand, stood against a cement pillar, waiting to board, completely and utterly alone.

Alone. Being alone had never really bothered me. I grew up the youngest child, which by nature left me to entertain myself while my older sisters got to do bigger and better things. This provided me ample time to invent a world of imaginary friends and fictional roles with which to amuse myself. Though my imaginary friends deserted me some time ago, I credit those formative years with the building of my imagination, where I have since spent countless hours living big and dreaming bigger. Sarah says I live my life like a character in my own movie, and in lots of ways I suppose she's right. It can be a bad thing, but it has definitely enabled me to remain satisfied and unafraid on my own—until now.

As I stood waiting to board my flight, I chased my loneliness away with thoughts of love. Perhaps I'd meet someone handsome and exciting on the flight. Perhaps we'd be seated next to each other, and fall in love before landing. After all, romance, like Paris, is *always* a good idea.

I scoped the male audience for lone travelers, imagining which one should coincidentally be assigned to seat 27E, right next to my 27F, so that we could spend the next nine hours engulfed in fascinating conversation. *Vive l'amour!* Unfortunately, the only remotely attractive man was ineligible for a plane-ride romance, as his arms were wrapped securely around a statuesque female, complete with a Rock of Gibraltar–size diamond weighing down her most important finger.

I was snapped out of my reverie by the flight attendant

calling first-class passengers. As Fabio escorted his diamond-dripping beauty through the gate toward the plane, I was seized with panic. Grabbing my cell phone—the one last touchstone to my family and friends—I scrolled through my phone to Sarah's number. Her number was programmed as "Nitty", sort of a childhood nickname that stuck. I punched the call button, holding my breath as it rang and rang on the other end. Nitty, my voice of reason—I needed desperately for her to pick up and say, *"Rachel, you'll be great! You've got everything you need."*

"You have reached the cell phone of Sarah Spencer . . ." Her voicemail came on instead. No last-minute lifesaver. No more touchstones to familiar voices. I sighed and left a message anyway. And that was it. With a leap of faith, I turned my cell phone off, knowing it would stay off for the next six weeks. I held down the power button, and watched the little good-bye icon appear, fade away, and sound its little good-bye jingle. Power off.

Of course I shouldn't have worried that I couldn't get through to Sarah. She'd already called at least five times to make sure I really did have everything I need. First, she called to make sure I had directions to the Vladescos' house in Paris. (I didn't.)

Next, she called to make sure I had adapters. (I thought I could buy some at the airport.)

Later, she asked me, "You've transferred some cash into euros, right?" (Sometimes it flatters me how high her expectations are.) Traveling is like Sarah's second job. The year-long stint when she worked as the Vladescos' nanny was just

Rachel Spencer

one of her many jaunts around the globe. She studied abroad in England in college. She backpacked through Europe after college graduation. I think she spent one summer doing the London-Paris-Rome thing. And it's not just Europe—she's been to Russia, Africa, Australia, pretty much everywhere. She's a teacher and in her classroom she has an entire doorway framed with patches of all the countries she's visited through the years. Originally she collected them because my mom said she would sew them on a backpack for Sarah. But I think they stayed in a plastic baggie on top of my mom's other sewing projects until Sarah found an alternative use for them. Sarah had always been the most industrious member of the family. I, on the other hand, tended to take after my mom, with projects galore stacked unfinished in piles throughout the house.

In fact, the first time I went to Paris for a high school trip, I realized the night before I was supposed to leave that my passport was missing. My mom and I spent half the night tearing through my room in a fruitless search. I went to school the next day ready to disappoint my French teacher, who had tediously planned the trip for our class, with the news that I couldn't go. Luckily, my mom called just in time to tell me she found the passport shoved inside the pages of my dictionary at home. I had always heard passports are very important documents that mustn't be lost or stolen, so I wanted to be sure I put it in a place that no one could find. Mission accomplished.

I've never been one for minor details. It's because of this that people like Sarah think I can't go anywhere by my-self. I may not be as organized, but somehow I get by just fine. Sure, she'd have a fit if she knew I left the directions to the Vladescos' at home. And if I told her I hadn't been to the ATM, she'd roll her eyes and sigh. Then when I clarified I had zero cash on me, let alone euros, she would probably lose her patience and exclaim, *"Rachel!"*

But there was one point on which I'd proven her wrong, and proven my luck. The adapters, I did manage to find. There's a Brookstone at the airport for people just like me.

I wanted to say *"Bonjour!"* to the airline agent scanning our boarding passes, but with her inch-long acrylic nails and over-processed frosted hair, she was clearly based out of Houston. Alas, my first French salutation would have to wait for Paris. As she pointed me toward my seat, she smiled warmly and I swear I detected some sort of comfort in her eyes. It was as if she knew I was heading toward something very unfamiliar. She probably saw girls like me all the time— boisterous, bubbly, ready to face the world, take the bull by the horns, and march into the great unknown! I smiled bravely back, feeling a twinge of excitement replace the panicked anxiety that had recently taken up residence in the pit of my stomach.

Even though seat 27E was occupied not by the man of my dreams, but by one of the fanny-packers (forget romance), we exchanged polite smiles in neighborly fashion. Time to buckle up. I couldn't quite visualize barging into the Vladescos' quaint family breakfast upon my morning arrival, but the stage was set, and the family was waiting, so it was *bonne journée* for me.

Croissant, anyone?

Rachel Spencer

* * *

Jet lag—what a drug. As the plane touched down at the Charles de Gaulle airport, I couldn't even begin to guess what the correct time was in Paris. I should've listened more carefully to the pilot's announcement and changed my watch with the rest of the cabin, but he was speaking in rapid-fire French, and I wasn't prepared for such immediate immersion.

The plane door opened to a gray and hazy morning. We exited directly onto the tarmac, and the romantic in me loved every minute of it. It was like stepping straight off the plane not just into a different country, but into a different time, a more charming time. As I bounded down the metal steps, I would not have been overly surprised to be greeted by a singing café waiter. I imagined him, in a red scarf and black beret, passing out hot croissants while serenading the arriving flight with his rendition of "La Vie en Rose." But I would have settled instead for a polite *"Bonjour!"* from the ground control crew, who waited at the bottom of the steps.

Sadly they were not as excited as I was about my arrival, and ignored my *"Bonjour"* and warm smile. In fact, I was entirely dismissed as they shooed me away from the plane and toward the airport entrance.

I couldn't be so easily discouraged. The air was heavy with foggy moisture. It made my first view of the sky less than picturesque, but *voilà*: it was *French* air, in a French sky. Through the clouds, I couldn't see the Eiffel Tower or any other sign of the city. But I knew it was out there. *Paris* was out there. And with it, boundless impending adventures.

Inside Charles de Gaulle, I scoured the signs for the

bathroom so I could freshen up and discovered that there were only two toilets for the hundreds of women pouring out of various international flights. Whose bright idea was that? I mean, I use two sinks in my daily getting-ready process and I'm only one person. How on earth are hordes of international women travelers supposed to accomplish necessary primping in such a space? Despite the limited facilities, I was, curiously enough, the only one interested in lugging my carry-on to the sink counter to peruse my selection of toiletries. Where were my fellow Texans? They probably found a bigger and better bathroom somewhere, but I had no notion to move now that I'd claimed a free sink. Free or not, I was surrounded by foreign faces and disheveled European women who were not entertained by my insistent effort to make myself at home in front of the public bathroom mirror. But I endured their glares and politely scooted my suitcase to one side whenever one of them deemed it appropriate to use the other sink. This was not often. Either they were too irritated to stand that closely to me, or more likely, washing hands is not part of their bathroom routine.

After fussing with my powder and hair and mascara for what seemed like forever, I faced the fact that there's only so much a girl can do to improve her appearance after a sleepless night, and I gave up. I had to get to baggage claim and find my way outside. I needed to get to the Vladescos', and though I now possessed a slightly improved physical appearance, I didn't want to arrive late.

It might have been the jet lag, or the Parisian humidity, or my overactive imagination, but my luggage felt considerably heavier in France than it had in America. Hauling my various suitcases along behind me as gracefully as I could, I set off for ground transportation. In one of her many sets of instructions, Sarah had informed me that the easiest way for me to get to the Vladescos' house was to take the Air France autobus that goes straight from the airport into Paris. Of course I had no idea how to get a ticket for this bus, and I hadn't asked her about it. If she'd figured it out on her own, so could I. Dragging about 150 pounds of suitcase behind me, I wandered back and forth looking for any type of desk that resembled Air France ground transportation. Jet lag consumed me like a drug at this point, and I knew that tears of frustration were not far behind. Thirty minutes and three information desks later I learned that you buy the passes once you're on the bus—which came every five minutes. *C'est la vie.*

I scrambled onto the next bus, tripping over my luggage, and collapsed into the nearest empty seat. Traffic on the *autoroute* was at a complete standstill and and I dozed off. Jet lag–induced sleep is like anesthesia, like severe delirium. One minute you're wide awake and the next everything turns into a hazy fog. Ahh, the welcome slumber! I faded in and out of coherence as we pushed through traffic.

Awake . . . drowsy . . . asleep . . . awake . . . drowsy . . . asleep. Some time later, I was jolted awake again by the intercom announcing something in French.

"Mmm," I purred, loving the sing-songy poetry of the language. "*L'Étoile—L'Arc de Triomphe,*" the voice said over the intercom. It sounded familiar, and at first, I couldn't figure out why.

"*L'Étoile—L'Arc de Triomphe,*" the intercom repeated.

"*L'Étoile?!*" I exclaimed to a man getting off the bus.

"*Oui!*" he confirmed.

That's when it hit me. *L'Étoile* wasn't just a pretty French word—it was my stop. I almost missed it! I grabbed my luggage, and wishing for a forklift, hauled my bags down onto the street corner. Gosh, it was hot outside. And where were we? I didn't see any l'Arc de Triomphe. "*Monsieur,*" I said to the man departing in front of me, "*Où est-ce que l'Arc de Triomphe?*"

He took me gingerly by the shoulders and turned me around to face a massive stone structure only yards away across the street. "*Voilà, mademoiselle!*" he said with a chuckle. Puzzled, I craned my neck upward to see the entirety of the structure. I stared for a few seconds more before realizing all that massive stone was one side of the Arc de Triomphe. This was Paris—this was my start—and I had finally arrived.

Walking from the bus stop to the Vladescos', I remembered the streets from the last time I saw Paris, about three years before. It was winter then, and the cafés that had been dark and shuttered against the winter elements were now bustling with animated faces and radiant crowds. Barren sidewalks that had been scattered with patches of dirt were now decorated with blossoms of all colors—tulips, lilies, roses and peonies, all the most beautiful flowers in the world. Along the streets, doors and windows were flung open to the warm air, the activity of the cafés and brasseries spilling out onto the sidewalks, where smiling summertime crowds lingered under large umbrella-shaded tables.

The city was louder than in winter. The café dwellers with their expressive conversations and gesturing hands displayed the celebration that is summer in Paris. I watched them talk, using as much body language as voice, squeezing as much expression as possible into the small spaces where they dined. As I walked, the sounds around me amplified. I heard gregarious guffaws rather than laughter, and saw dancing faces rather than mere stares. Small, funny-shaped European cars buzzed through the streets, with horns simultaneously triggered by the gas pedal. I could have stood and watched the spectacle all afternoon, but I pressed on with my bags in tow, feeling as if it were all a dream—a good dream and one from which I never wanted to wake.

On bike, rollerblades, and on foot, everyone enjoyed the sun. But laboring along with my luggage, I quickly became drenched in sweat. I'd hardly arrived and I already resented their blasé approach to life. Unaffected by heat, immune to perspiration—who *were* these people? The sunny skies did not match the haze of exhaustion that settled over me, and I wished for the gray skies I saw upon landing. I finally surrendered to the heat and pulled my hair, which by that time hung in damp clumps, into a tight ponytail, undoing all of the primping from the airport bathroom. Though it pained me, I was forced to relinquish my last effort to appear well groomed and professional upon greeting the family.

Not surprisingly, I forgot my way to the Vladescos'. Unlike the grid systems of the U.S., the streets in Paris are centered around little gardens, parks, or fountains, like roundabouts. The streets that branched out in every direction were at first glance dizzyingly similar. I thought about calling the Vladescos for help, but remembered I didn't have any cash, or their phone number. If Sarah knew, she would be giving me one of her *I told you so* looks. I ventured forward in faith. To remain positive, I tried taking in the scenery. To remain awake, I tried to concentrate on what I hoped was the proper direction. Every building appeared inviting, decked with tidy rows of perfect windows nestled behind tiny black cast-iron balconies. All of the windows had been flung open to the sunshine, and I couldn't help but feel that today, they were open to me. I thought of it as my own personal welcome gift from Paris.

Boulevard Pereire was my destination, and I searched up and down the streets for the right sign. In Paris, there were no street signs nailed to poles at the intersections. Instead, the street names were labeled on simple address plaques mounted for subtle view on every corner building, only if needed and only if the passing pedestrians were interested. It was just another way the city was romantic in everything it does. Just as I thought I had taken the wrong route, I spotted the sign for Boulevard Pereire—mostly covered by the leaves of a tree. And after a right turn and a few more steps, I arrived in front of number 37. I had found my way.

I stood for a few minutes, breathing in and out in front of the bright peacock-blue double-doored entry, which stood as the face to the Vladescos' four-story townhouse. It was a grandiose entrance, flanked on either side by thick stone sconces and crowned on top with lavishly carved stone. To the right of the door was a tastefully concealed intercom system, complete with a little gold button—a button that I was, after airport primping, transportation confusion, traffic jams, and pedestrian meandering, beyond late to press. I took one more deep breath, brushed the sweat off my forehead, reached out my finger toward the little gold button, and pushed.

Chapitre Deux

"*Allô?*" a voice called through the intercom. Even through the speaker, the voice was poised and refined. I guessed it was Estelle, the mother of the Vladesco household.

"Hi, it's Rachel. I'm here," I chirped, wincing at the sound of my own voice. If I was trying to match Estelle's cool tone, I'd already blown my cover.

The blue door jarred open to reveal three of the five Vladescos—Estelle, Léonie, and Constantin. Constantin, the youngest and the family's only son, stood in the doorway, closest to me.

"Hi," I said. "Constantin?"

He didn't answer. Instead, he openly looked me up and down with a snobbish judgment more like that of a grown Frenchman than a seven-year-old boy. He furrowed his brow, taking in my sweaty, blue jean–clad appearance, and delivered his calculated results with a precocious half-turned smile. I waited for him to blurt out a one-word summary, but he kept his expression, with his judgment, fixed on his face as my smile faded in his stare.

Not to be intimidated, I looked toward Léonie, the middle child, who stood on the steps of the stone entryway. She stood shyly between her brother and Estelle with a gaze kinder and softer than Constantin's. I could tell she was thinking, though I didn't know what. She had a pensive smile, and I understood from it we would get along just fine.

"Hi, Léonie," I said.

Before she could reply, Estelle stepped forward, grinning coolly, and whisked Léonie to her side.

"Welcome, Rachel," Estelle said. She kept her hand on Léonie's shoulder.

"Hi," I said. I nudged my bags forward.

With a casual nod of the head, she shooed her children along and gestured me inside.

"Come in," she said, and closed the door behind me.

The lights were off inside the house, and the sunlight cast shadows through the windows. I was relieved to be in the midst of air-conditioning and instantly felt a chill as the sweat cooled on my skin.

"Your plane was delayed?" Estelle asked, incorrectly assuming that my tardiness was a result of the airlines. I glanced at my watch, which was still on Houston time, and added seven hours. I was about two hours past my expected arrival time. I wanted to lie and blame the airlines, which would have been an easy alibi. But dishonesty wasn't the best foundation to lay for the next six weeks of caring for her children.

"No," I replied. "We landed right on time, but I got

lost in the airport, and had trouble buying my AirFrance bus ticket."

"You buy the tickets on the bus, *non?*" Estelle asked. Her tone was innocent enough, but I felt foolish in my mistake just the same. Still, I smiled and nodded my head, desperate to get off on the right foot. I had no way of knowing it at the time, but that gesture would become my ultimate defense mechanism for the remainder of the trip: When in doubt, smile and nod.

Constantin and Léonie politely took my bags up the front entry steps to the main floor, and Estelle, gracious and forgiving of my tardiness, motioned for me to follow her to the kitchen. Even though it was still early in the afternoon, I could have gone to sleep right then and there. I was nearly shaking from exhaustion and this was hardly the way I'd intended to make my first impression. But I didn't exactly have a free night at the Ritz to refresh and rejuvenate beforehand. So I tightened my ponytail and followed Estelle, observing the surroundings of my new home.

Here in the grandeur of the Vladesco house, the windows welcomed me just as grandly as those I'd seen on every building walking from the bus stop. Opening in pairs, they were easily the height of a normal door, but leaner because in Paris, a window, like most anything else, was nothing short of a tall and elegant beauty. The windows were drawn open, revealing the world outside—the blue sky, the sweet summer air, the bright green of trees and vines that decorated the Vladescos' private garden patio. The June breeze swept in and out, blending the air of two worlds into one. The air was clean, sweet, and easy, playfully ruffling the regal canary-colored draperies that billowed to the floor below in pools of rich fabric. A sliding glass door that ran the length of the back kitchen wall opened to the outside patio, which sported a rather grand wooden patio table and chairs, covered by a large, shaded umbrella. From the remains on the table, it looked as though the family had already eaten, *sans* tardy nanny. Estelle pointed me through the door to the patio table where they'd left an empty place setting for me.

The garden, as the Vladescos called it, was a tiny wood-decked triangle of land that I, as a suburban-dwelling American, would have called merely a patio or a courtyard, to be romantic at best. However, in Paris, it was equivalent to real estate gold to come upon any residential property with a private outdoor area. It took me a while to realize this. Alex, the father and resident chef, was particularly proud of his garden. And in the summertime, the grill was his outdoor kitchen. Years ago, Sarah boasted of Alex's culinary displays and when I visited, I tasted them for myself. We ate wild boar with cranberry relish; hearty, meaty potatoes of all sorts; wild mushrooms—dark, woodsy things. But of course after three years and many seasons past, I'd forgotten the wonderment of Alex's gourmet goldmine. Quickly, I remembered. And quickly I realized that, as evidenced by the sliding glass door opened from the kitchen to the garden, and the lid of the grill sitting sideways on the ground to cool, Alex had increased his domain since my winter visit. He had progressed with the seasons from hunter to gardener. I stood in front of the table piled with half-filled platters and nearly empty bowls, all brightly colored mixes of the season's freshest recipes. It was the first introduction I had—and one of many—to the savory seasonings of summer in the garden, *chez Vladesco*.

Just as I sat down, I noticed the reclined chef, resting in a lounge chair *au soleil*. His smug expression, pursed lips, and squinted eyes told me he was satisfied, if not uncomfortably full, from his lunchtime symphony of grilled meat-and-vegetable kebabs.

"Oh, Alex!" I said. "I didn't see you at first. How are you?"

"Cooking," he murmured without opening his eyes or even raising his head. And that was the end of our exchange.

With one word, Alex taught me an important lesson in French manners and culture—or in the manners and culture of Alex, I should say, which would prove more important to me than that of the country as a whole. In the South, polite small talk is an integral part of a meal, or of any exchange. In France, Alex's terse reply taught me it was not appropriate to interrupt a man during his meal, and especially inappropriate to interrupt the resting period that follows. Visiting—completely welcomed. Interruption—deplorable. It was clear that Alex was not in the mood for visiting. I served myself and chewed in silence, while Alex rested off to the side, continuing his "cooking," which by then resembled nothing more than miserable sweating.

As I helped Estelle tidy the kitchen after lunch, I realized someone was missing. At fourteen years old, Diane was the oldest of the Vladesco children and the lone teenager. I was looking forward to spending time with her. She was too old to need me in the traditional "nanny" sense, but I thought maybe I could become her friend in a big sister kind of way.

"Diane's not home?" I asked Estelle.

Estelle continued scraping bell pepper and carrot off the dirty plates and into the trashcan. "I wonder why she hasn't come down," she replied, arching her eyebrows and turning the corners of her mouth upward into a wry smile. I couldn't tell if she smiled to cover slight embarrassment or irritation. Part of me believed her to be humored by the situation, which I didn't understand at all. But Estelle was a French woman, and French women never tell their secrets.

As if to illustrate Estelle's point, the telephone rang, but just as she reached for it, it stopped ringing. She shrugged and gave me that smile again, but I understood it this time. "*Teenagers*," the smile said. A few minutes later, as we were drying the dishes, Diane rounded the corner into the kitchen and smiled with awkward excitement, as she was of the age when it's not cool to show too much emotion of any kind. I was struck by how adult she looked. The last time I'd seen her, she was eleven, and though beautiful then, still very much a little girl. But she had since grown into a tall, lithe beauty. Her long, glossy hair fell straight down her back. She had her father's mouth, with his full lips. Her eyes though, were Estelle's, accentuated by prominent arched, dark eyebrows. And though she was young, her eyes were cunning, and full of the secrets of a French woman. As I swept her in for a hug, I couldn't help but wonder what sorts of secrets she was keeping behind those eyes, and the twinge of nerves I'd felt a few minutes before turned into a surge of intimidation. The girl was nine years my junior, yet her look, her manners, even her movements, were more grown up than mine. I could handle the youthful exuberance of Léonie and Constantin, but could I handle the turbulent hormones of a fourteen-year-old?

By the time the six of us sat down to dinner at eight o'clock— very European—I was nearly dead on my feet. Throughout the dinner, I had the chance to observe the Vladescos and each of their mannerisms. I sat next to Alex, the king of the table, who presided proudly over the meal, guiding the conversation. He took it upon himself to give me detailed lessons on the origin of each and every food on the table, and I indulged him.

Estelle said little throughout dinner, looking content and entertained, appreciating the evening. She was like a puzzle I couldn't quite figure out, and compared to her, I felt too fast, too dramatic—too *American*. Constantin sat on my left, tugging my arm for a *goûter*—or taste—*du vin* throughout dinner. To my surprise, all three kids were offered a *goûter* before the night's end. They politely took the few sips they were given, smacking their lips together and smiling with guilty pleasure.

I pinned my eyelids open long enough to say *"Merci et bonsoir"* to my new *famille* and off I went to the bliss of slumber. In my nanny room, two deep-ledged, boxy windows opened to street level. I lay my dinnertime clothes, damp from my tired body and a dewy warm evening on the patio, on the window ledge. As I climbed into bed, I glanced at my watch, still on Houston time. The digital clock by the bed read military time as did all clocks in France, and my jet-lagged brain couldn't even begin to calculate what time it was. It flashed some number in the twenties but I closed my eyes to avoid thinking further. Whatever the time, it was still early for Paris as sounds of whirring car tires and honking horns polluted the evening air. Sounds of the city, and I loved it.

Morning greeted me with several unpleasant surprises. First, I woke up in the middle of a full-blown allergy attack. Whenever I experience a weather change or should my sleep pattern be disturbed my body responds with dripping sinuses, itching eyes, and compulsive sneezing. And lucky me, I was currently experiencing all of the above. *Avez-vous un tissue?*

I shrugged it off and proceeded to the shower, hoping a little hot steam would alleviate my symptoms. But as I undressed, I discovered an entirely different problem. I was dotted all over with bumps. My arms, chest, legs, and even my stomach were plagued with strange little beads. They had an odd resemblance to beads of condensation on a water glass, but they felt more like bubbles of skin. *Delicious*, I thought. *What was this? Dehydration?* Whatever the cause, it was a less than desirable condition in which to start my first day as a nanny.

Despite waking up a snot-nosed, ogre-like leper, I tried to keep a positive attitude, turning my attention to the more pressing matter of this *très* important first day on the job. Lest I forsake my personal recipe for success, I approached the most important task: dressing the part. I strategically planned an *ensemble parfait* for the combative duties undoubtedly associated with an au pair's mission.

My black button-down shirtdress, tailored and *très chic,* showed that I had style while proving I wasn't afraid to get my freshly manicured hands dirty. Although I had to admit it would be a shame when my OPI "Sweetheart" polish chipped. But I felt confident the black button-down would enable me to march through a hectic first-day agenda looking well equipped for the task, whether or not the polish stayed. I also knew that my choice of shoe would give the outfit even more pump and panache. I considered for a moment pairing the ensemble with my Kate Spade zebra stripes with four-inch heels and a black leather ankle strap. *Incroyable, je sais.* But they were probably better suited for an evening out at the Hemingway bar than a day caring for three children.

So I opted instead for my more practical gold flip-flops. Ha! My day's work hadn't even begun, and already I'd chosen the kids' best interest over mine. What a good-hearted, selfless, thoughtful, loving, concerned nanny! I finished the look with a neatly coiffed ponytail and accessorized with tortoise-shell jewelry—an effort to enhance my safari glam vibe. Considering the jungle I was getting myself into, I wanted to be dressed for combat. Then it hit me, *besides the outfit, how was I really prepared for this battle?*

After all, my track record didn't exactly shout nanny

material. So I don't really know why I thought being one was a good idea. I've certainly never been the prototype for governess, as recounted in my unofficial nanny résumé.

1. Babysitting Experience. Growing up I was definitely not the babysitter of choice among the neighborhood moms. It was like an unspoken conspiracy against me, but it was there. I probably wouldn't have noticed it at all if the various moms hadn't chosen Sarah—always responsible, always organized Sarah—over me for the job.

"Why won't they ask *me* to baby-sit?" I'd whine to my mother.

"Well, Sarah's older, honey," my mom would remind me. As if that was any reason for her to get asked instead of me. "Besides," she'd say. "They've asked you before, but you're always busy."

My mom was kind to appease me. But this part was a complete lie, and my mom and I both knew it. I mean, the number of Friday nights I spent at home in high school was just downright embarrassing. Not that spending them babysitting would have been cool, but it would have been cooler than staying home.

And it was good money. I mean, depending on the number of kids and the neighborhood, babysitting could easily pay 20 dollars an hour. And that was a much more lucrative business than some store clerk position that paid minimum wage—not that I did that either.

However, like most jobs that involve caring for other human beings, the people who are truly called to do it aren't looking at the lucrative advantages. The best babysitters, the ones parents love, actually love the kids and love taking care of them. Like Sarah.

It's not that I don't love people. I've always been a people person. It's just not evident in my work, that's all. Which leads me to recount the one time I actually *did* babysit.

Right after I graduated college (that's right, I was twenty-one before parents started trusting me alone with small children), I got my first gig. There was about a month-long period while I sat at home waiting for an offer from the *Chronicle*. I was extremely depressed because my friends were still having the time of their life in college and I was back in my hometown with no job and absolutely nothing to do. So when my mom volunteered me to babysit one day, I was grateful. It was like a ray of hope for me. Maybe, despite the damaging years of babysitting rejection in high school, I was the nurturing type, after all. I couldn't wait to rub it in to Sarah, who happened to be in Houston at the time as well.

So I woke up at the crack of dawn on the day of the job, already a virtuous sacrifice in my opinion, and drove out to the babysitting house. Score—it was totally huge. Even though I was only watching one kid, I figured this could definitely be a 20-dollar-per-hour gig—especially because the kid was a toddler, and they're just so much more work. Once inside, the house looked like even more work than the toddler, whose name I can't remember. This was slightly disheartening, as I had anticipated using the day for a vacation of sorts, pretending I was on retreat from my parents' house. But alas, the house was in shreds and the little guy was in the middle of it. I hadn't the slightest clue what to do with him, but to prove to myself and to parents across the world that my babysitting capabilities were sorely underappreciated, I decided to clean the house. I stuck the little guy in one of those Fisher-Price swing things with a lap tray so kids can swing and eat and stay generally entertained, and I got to work, humming along to the local oldies stations. No need to debilitate a child's budding intellect with that Barney nonsense, right? Apparently the kid didn't appreciate my taste in music, though, because he screamed bloody murder the whole time.

I gave up cleaning—there are only so many Cheerios you can handpick off someone else's kitchen floor before you feel like vomiting anyway—and decided we should watch a movie together. At first I thought we could both curl up on the couch, but he was kind of small, and I was a little worried about accidentally crushing him—so I put him on the floor. There were lots of toys down there for him anyway and it's not like he could really run off anywhere. I found one of those made-for-TV Lifetime movies that can be really therapeutic if you're in the mood. And something about it reminded me of when I was a little kid home sick from school. So I figured it was great for the little guy because it would imprint similar warm memories on his childhood. I knew one day he could look back on this very moment and remember how fondly he was loved.

I awakened an undetermined amount of time later to see my sister Sarah standing above me, half laughing and half shouting in disbelief at my lack of responsibility. I wasn't sure if she stopped by to keep me company or to make sure I wasn't burning the place down.

Sarah's foul temper got the kid crying all over again. But instead of being annoyed by his crying like me, she swooped him up off the floor and asked me when I'd last changed his diaper.

"Umm . . . Does he wear diapers?" I said. I was sort of lying—I knew he wore diapers, but was unable to admit I hadn't quite gotten around to changing him.

From that point on, Sarah took over while I ordered a pizza and baked us cookies. They turned out *really* well but Sarah never even thanked me. It's so hard to work with ungrateful people.

2. *Nutrition*. I had horrible eating habits, as evidenced by my aforementioned penchant for baking and eating pizza and cookies in times of crisis. But I was certain I'd be great when it came to the Vladesco children and their nutrition. At least I hoped I would.

The only time I was ever responsible for the care and feeding of another living thing for a prolonged period of time was with Aspen, my cat. I bought Aspen on a whim the summer after my freshman year in college. I was working full time in my first ad sales job (why I didn't figure out then that ad sales was not for me remains a mystery and thus supports my inability to learn from bad experiences). I thought I would love the job and spend my evenings living it up with my friends. But I hated the job and ended up going home exhausted every night. So I got bored fast and, one day during my lunch break, went by the local animal shelter. I guess I thought buying an animal for companionship would be better than eating for companionship. I fell in love with a kitten there, paid for her, and took her home. I named her Aspen because she looked snowy—white and fluffy with icy blue eyes and ears that were just barely tipped with gray. I've also always wanted to go to Aspen and thought it sounded cool to own a cat by that name.

Aspen was so cute and tiny when she was a baby, even her meow sounded small. I know it's weird, but I kind of wanted to keep her that way. It's so sad when animals grow from cute babies into boring adults. And there's nothing you can do about it. The vet recommended IAMS cat food for Aspen to strengthen her bones and help her grow, but that sounded dry and way too serious for my ski resort kitty. So I came up with my own diet. You know, just a little whatever here and there—but I made sure we always took our meals together, a true sign of my family values. There were several occasions when I ordered double meat on my Subway cold cuts so that I could share it with my darling little Aspen. And when I made pancakes on the weekend, I always made extra for her. I even served it to her on little crystal plates. I really loved her. So I can safely and truthfully say it was never my intention to undernourish her.

My friends would come over and say, "She's still so small!" or "She's so cute and little!" "I know," I would say back. "She's *dainty*." I was so proud of Aspen for being such a tiny cat. Until Sarah came to visit.

Unlike my friends, Sarah was not impressed that my cat had only gained one pound in six months. She didn't think it was cute and she didn't think I was cute. She warned me that I was starving my cat and could not be convinced otherwise, even when I told her how generous I was with my double meat Subways. She also suggested that the reason Aspen meowed so much was *not* because she knew I thought it sounded cute. She meowed because she was hungry. I found that hard to believe because just that morning I'd given her a slice of French toast with extra cranberry-raspberry sauce. (It was one of my favorite recipes from my *Betty Crocker Home for the Holidays* cookbook.)

Despite Sarah's protestations, I still think Aspen loved to meow because she, like me, thought it sounded cute. We were the best of friends—really—but I had to give her away when I moved to my next college residence. She lives on a farm now, where I'm sure she probably misses her crystal plates and water dishes and where she's probably very upset with the inevitable weight gain that comes with country living.

3. Driving Record. Okay, so I got a ticket the first day I got my license. But I mean, who hasn't gotten a ticket at least once in their life? It's so harsh to make a sixteen-year-old feel like a criminal, especially on her birthday. I'm not saying sixteen is too early to administer driver's licenses to teenagers, I'm just saying no matter when you get the license, there should be a buffer zone.

Now that I've had plenty of experience, I've learned

what it takes to talk my way out of a ticket. This really is a skill they *don't* teach in Driver's Ed and that few possess. Some people (read: Sarah) have hinted that my level of experience must mean I'm a bad driver. But those people are probably just jealous because they *can't* talk their way out of tickets. Also, I'm very appreciative every time an officer lets me off the hook. I always thank them several times for their understanding. Most recently, I went a little over the top and actually shook his hand while gushing, *"Oh, thank you, officer!"* He seemed shocked but appreciative, nonetheless.

Wrecks are a different subject. There's no talking your way out of them and they are very expensive mistakes. So I've honed my powers of persuasion here while convincing my insurance company they shouldn't drop me. It's very important to understand the value of this relationship and I do. Austin Whitfield at State Farm is a really nice guy. I wouldn't go so far as to say he's "like a good neighbor," but he hasn't dropped me yet, and that's good enough for me.

Fortunately, though, my driving record isn't really relevant to my position as an au pair because I will not be driving in Paris. The Vladesco family thought it would be a hassle for me, and I am grateful for their thoughtfulness; there are apparently *a lot* of bad drivers in Paris, and I wouldn't want to expose myself or the children to such danger.

4. Punctuality. Okay, I'm never *intentionally* late. It's just that there always seem to be numerous extenuating circumstances that keep me from being punctual. Always. I'm just not one of those left-brained people who live by their clocks. I know that tardiness is rude. But when you think about it, *punctuality* is such an ugly word. Really, say it out loud: "punctual." It sounds ugly, doesn't it?

Ugly or not, this punctuality thing is *très* relevant for making a good first-day-on-the-job impression. So I shook myself loose of past resume experiences and marched upstairs to add more to my list, ready or not.

Chapitre Trois

I pranced to the kitchen at 8 a.m., a regular Mary Poppins. I was practically singing "A Spoonful of Sugar" as I rummaged through the breakfast cabinet Estelle had pointed out the day before. From the contents of their breakfast cabinet, one would never guess that Estelle and all three children are model-thin. The cabinet is stocked with all manner of sugary breakfast items, from Nesquik, *miel de lavande* (a buttery yellow, viscous honey peculiar to France), and a variety of *confitures*, to the most sugary-sweet of all American cereals—Cocoa Puffs and Frosted Flakes. The cabinet also contained the world's largest collection of ceramic espresso cups and mini saucers, presumably to be filled by the very expensive-looking espresso machine on the counter below, with which I planned to become very familiar. I was unable to find any bread on which to spread the *miel et confiture,* so I put out the cereal, milk, and some Nesquik and greeted the little darlings one by one as they stumbled into the kitchen with adorably sleepy eyes.

But the kids only picked at their food before leaving the table again, presumably to get ready for school. I was a little deflated, but tried to go with the flow of the household. I cleaned up after them, pouring three full bowls of milk and cereal down the drain, pushing puffs through the drain cracks, and wiping down the steel sink until it sparkled. The next time I glanced at the clock, it was 8:25, leaving me only five minutes to get the kids to school. I was desperate to run the household with the same effortless grace as Estelle, or at least with the efficiency of Mary Poppins, yet already I was behind schedule. Get it together, Rachel, I said to myself as I headed toward the door.

By the time I got to the top of the entryway stairs, Estelle, Constantin, and Léonie were waiting for me by the door. Estelle had promised to lead the way to school for future reference, and I was grateful I wouldn't have to wander the streets alone with two children in tow. I looked around for Diane, but she was nowhere to be seen. She probably had her own separate routine to follow.

As I descended the staircase, I thought again about how smart I'd been to choose the gold flip-flops over the Kates, as I surely would have broken my neck trying to hurry down such a slippery staircase in four-inch heels. And then— *whoops*—my sandal skidded on the slick stone and before I knew it, I was sailing through the air. I landed spread-eagle at the bottom of the staircase, baring all to the Vladesco family in my *très chic* black dress.

Constantin, Léonie, and Estelle gathered around me, their eyes wide. I'd lost a flip-flop on the way down, and Constantin rushed to retrieve it for me.

"Your shoe?!" he said, his voice full of concern, and I

took it from his tiny hand, grateful for his hospitality and touched by his careful attention.

"Are you alright?" Estelle asked politely.

Léonie just stared at me in horror. She was just old enough to be embarrassed by such an immodest fall. And I was just young enough to want to die from such a terrible first-day fate. But I couldn't let her know that.

"I'm fine," I said, brushing dirt and a layer of my pride off the backside of my dress. "Really. I'm ready to go!" I said, keeping my voice bright.

I skulked my way to school, following just a few steps behind the dynamic Vladesco trio. With one hand, Estelle smoothed Léonie's flyaway hairs from the base of her neck, and with the other, she held on to Constantin, who skipped along, looking lovingly up at her. I watched them walk ahead, a perfect family picture, while rubbing my sore bottom and wondering where—if ever—I could fit into the frame. When we finally arrived at school, I waved and flashed my "nanni-est" smile while Estelle kissed the kiddies good-bye. Then they disappeared through the school gates with all of the other children, eager and busy and buzzing with the promise a new day brings. Estelle turned to me. "Okay. Enjoy Paris!" she said, before turning on her heel and striding off down the street. I watched till she faded from view, becoming just another face in the Monday morning crowd shuffling along the dirty Paris sidewalks. That's when I realized that I hadn't paid attention to how we'd gotten there. I had no idea how to get home—or how I would find my way back to pick up the kids that afternoon.

I was completely alone. In Paris. It was a prospect that both frightened and thrilled me. I had eight luxurious hours before I had to pick the children up from school, and for a moment, I fantasized about spending all of them walking the streets of Paris. But alas, Estelle had work for me to do at the house, so I turned in the direction that I hoped would lead me home.

With so many winding streets and tall buildings in Paris, it's easy for a newcomer to get confused, and I nearly walked straight past the peacock blue doors of the Vladesco house. After struggling with the door key no fewer than three times, I finally make it back inside.

The house felt different with just me in it, and I stood in the entryway for several moments, taking it all in. It even smelled different. I hadn't noticed a smell before. Either that or the house was full of other people smells and food smells, and taking those in was occupation enough for a newcomer. Soft light shone through the kitchen skylights onto the polished hardwood floors, but it was cool inside. I could have fallen asleep.

Every room of the house was immaculate, save for the kitchen, where the Vladescos really lived. The kitchen smelled different from the rest of the house, a combination of day-old trash, morning milk, freshly ground espresso beans, and the piquant whiff of whatever cheeses lurked behind the closed refrigerator doors. I was actually impressed the cheeses were kept within the confines of the refrigerator. Three years ago when I'd visited, the cheeses were kept out on the counter,

Rachel Spencer

and I learned pasteurization was not nearly as popular in France as in America. But maybe cheese on the counter was a winter thing. Who could tell?

Above all the smells, the espresso called to me' the most. Beckoned me. Lured me. Sang to me with its chocolaty, nutty undertones. The sweet aroma drew me to the counter, where the half-pound brown bag from Brulerie des Ternes sat tucked in the crevice between the breakfast cabinet and the gleaming espresso machine. I had the feeling that machine would become one of my closest friends this summer. There are two words in the American language that are highly over-looked. Words that are taken for granted, or lumped in with other tasks. But there in the mid-morning presence of a coffee connoisseur's fantasy machine, I vowed from that moment forward to always savor deeply the true meaning of the phrase "coffee break."

It was high time I indulged myself in a hot double shot of espresso, courtesy of the Vladescos' espresso machine. The machine was beyond high-tech, with a price tag that eas-ily exceeded 2000 dollars, no doubt. To the Vladescos, the heavenly liquid that poured out of the machine every morn-ing was merely *un café*. But to me, it was nothing short of the strongest, purest, finest espresso I'd ever had in my life. I scanned through the digital menu, desperate to take the machine out for a test drive. The first step said something about size, so I pressed the double shot button. But somehow I got it wrong and instead of making coffee, I merely changed the language on the machine. It might have been Russian. I pressed the same button again and the language switched to

Swahili. I continued button-pushing, hoping the thing didn't malfunction and/or turn off, until—*voilà!* The machine rumbled to life, filling the room with the sound and heady scent of grinding beans. It beeped at me and spit a bit and then, out came my ink. I sighed and inhaled the rich aroma. Such satisfaction and I hadn't even brought the cup to my lips.

But this was no time for a simple repast—this coffee break had to be accompanied by some serious nanny planning. Across the kitchen, on the steel island countertop, set discreetly to the side of family paper stacks and the telephone, there lay a book. I'd avoided it until now, but it was time. I took a swig of espresso for courage.

Estelle called it the diary; I called it the nanny book. It was a small, canvas-bound book that lived in the top drawer of the island in the Vladesco kitchen. But make no mistake; the hidden nature of the nanny book did not undermine its vital role in a nanny's life. Every day, Estelle wrote within it the household schedules, chores, menus, and errands. My job meant following these notes to the letter.

It was somewhat reassuring that in a house so unapologetically modern, and with two parents who were fully reliant on whichever Palm Pilot or Blackberry was the most up to date, the family's affairs were still penned by hand on the dated pages of a little canvas diary. The nanny book was a reflection of the way Estelle expected her household to be run—efficiently, elegantly, and without incident.

Nestled discreetly next to the nanny book's place in the drawer was the house purse. Should there be an errand like running to the market for several meals' worth of produce, the amount needed to purchase such produce would be in the house purse. The house purse was separated into two sides—one for coins and one for bills. The coins were for buying the daily baguettes. The side containing the bills was full or empty, depending on the errands listed in the nanny book for that day. I sipped my darling cocktail again and read what was expected from me the first day on the job.

Un rétro—buy for breakfast. I had no idea what a *rétro* was, but realized with dread that *un rétro* would have supplied the base we were missing for the *miel et confiture* at this morning's breakfast table. How was I to know what *un rétro* was—and moreover, how was I to know where to buy one?!

"*Drink elixir,*" my brain told me, and I considered filling a second cup. Unlike lattes, which require a certain amount of lingering over, espresso was quick. And the best part was, comparatively speaking, this stuff was *sans* Starbucks price tag and virtually calorie-free.

Empowered, I read on.

> *Constantin needs glasses fixed. Take to l'Opticien. 14, rue Benjamin Franklin.*
> *Buy 1 kilo cherries, 2 courgettes, 1 aubergine, 3 tomates (10E).*
> *Pick up kids from school at 16h30.*
> *Supper:*
> > *Quiche*
> > *Salade (use tomato bought at market)*
> > *Yoghurt or Fruit*

Estelle was completely fluent in French and English, and browsing through past nanny book entries, I noted that I'd be reading both languages. If I'd had an extensive French vocabulary, or at least a basic knowledge of French produce, this wouldn't have been a problem. But I didn't, so it was a problem. I made a mental note to explore the fascinating world of French produce where the elusive *courgettes* and *aubergines* lived—whatever they were—along with the more familiar *cherries* and *tomates*.

And what of *l'opticien*? Not only did I *not* know that Constantin wore glasses, but I also had no idea how to find my way to rue Benjamin Franklin. To make matters worse, my French was a little rusty (read: nonexistent). *Cassé—c'est le mot* for "broke," *non*?

And the cooking of the quiche? Well, that just wasn't a task I dared consider before nine o'clock in the morning.

As the espresso took effect, I began to feel better. My morning stair-tumble seemed a million miles away, I felt thinner already as a result of my new all-caffeine diet, and despite a little dust on the backside, my dress was still *très chic*. It was time to say *bonjour* to Paris. I pranced out the door with nanny book and necessary euros clutched in hand, confident that *le métro* would not be as scary as it seemed.

Estelle had informed me that I needed to buy *"un carnet,"* which would buy me ten tickets on *le métro*. To reach rue Benjamin Franklin and *l'opticien*, I had to take the line to La Place Trocadéro, near the Eiffel Tower. I had seen the tip of the Eiffel Tower peeking out from a distance while walking near the Champs, so I knew it wasn't far. However, I couldn't find a direct *métro* route that would take me to it. After careful scrutiny of the map, I found *ligne C* with a stop at Champ de Mars, which looked like an alternative route to the Eiffel Tower. Surely I could walk from there to La Place Trocadéro. Well, surely I could walk to Russia from there, too, but why do things the easy way? And with that, I chose *ligne C*.

I'd expected to board a dirty, fluorescent-lit, run-down train, and was pleasantly surprised when a rather new two-level train with SNCF written on the side pulled into the station. I thought I remembered the SNCF from my first trip to Paris. Hadn't I taken it to Nice? Hmmm. I boarded anyway, glancing at my watch. Six hours to spare before picking up the kids again. Surely if I was on the wrong train, I could get off before Nice and turn around, right? Right. I stared out the window at my reflection, hardly able to believe my new world. Just two weeks ago on a Monday morning, I would have been bustling through the *Houston Chronicle* offices, with sales goals and deadlines and reports piling up on my desk. And for a brief moment, I missed it. I didn't know where I was; I didn't know where I was going. I didn't know what was to come. It was scary, but it had to be better than wasting away in my cubicle, dreaming of another life.

When the train pulled into the next stop there was no sign indicating where we were. I waited for the overhead announcement to clarify the stop. No announcement. A few people around me gathered their things and disembarked. I wanted to ask them, *"How in the world do you know where you're going?!"* But before I could summon either the courage or the correct vocabulary, the train resumed motion. If only I'd bought a *métro* map—but that would have called me out as a tourist, and the last thing I wanted to be mistaken for was a tourist.

I went back to staring out the window, perfecting my blasé, unaffected, and *très* French look, when I noticed a true Parisian intensely studying the full route of *ligne C* posted above the train doors. Every last stop was marked, and I counted the stops to Champ de Mars, only four stops away. I was pleased that I'd found the right train, but slightly disappointed that Nice would have to wait.

The stop at Champ de Mars was bordered to the left by La Seine. I wound my way through the gardens, sprinklers, and sidewalks toward Trocadéro, using the tip of the Eiffel Tower as my guide. It was a picture-perfect summer morning in Paris. The sun was bright in the sky, and the buttery aroma of fresh croissants hung in the air, beckoning me. But I was determined to find rue Benjamin Franklin and accomplish my first official nanny task before indulging myself.

I followed the delicious smell until I reached the base of the Eiffel Tower. I walked beneath it, side-stepping the tourists and chuckling softly at my good fortune. I'd escaped the gloom of Monday morning paperwork, phone calls, and meetings, and replaced it with jaunting through the gardens of Paris. By the time I found Rue Benjamin Franklin, it was 11 o'clock, it was hot, I was starving, and I couldn't wait to sit down in the air conditioned doctor's office. I wandered down the street, searching for the right building. What a strange co-incidence that the optician's office was on rue Benjamin

Franklin. As I scanned the building numbers, I wondered if they specialized in bifocals.

I was scouring the little numbered plaques above the doors when it dawned on me that all of the buildings on the street looked closed or abandoned. In fact, every building and office on the street sported pull-down gates and blackened windows . . . including number fourteen. I stood in front of *l'opticien*'s dark window for a long time, eyeing a pair of square-framed Chanels and imaging how they would go with my current ensemble, and wondering what to do next. Then I noticed a sign posted on the door: *L'Opticien Fermé. Ouvrier a 14h Lundi.*

Great. I didn't have time to wait for three hours until it opened or I'd be late picking the children up from school. And I had yet to buy the produce for dinner. So *l'opticien* would have to wait. And thus I learned my first lesson in Parisian business hours: Mondays are about as good as a weekend for running errands, and weekends are a complete bust. Establishments such as doctor's offices typically don't open for full business hours until Tuesday.

I reasoned that since *l'opticien* was crossed off of my list for the day, I had time for a long-overdue and well-deserved visit to the nearest patisserie for a rest, a snack, and a glass of water. Though most of the shops were closed, I happened upon an inviting storefront on a side street with the words *"Salon du Thé"* stenciled in an arch across the shop window. I walked in and smiled weakly at the hosetess. *"Pour une, s'il-vous-plaît,"* I said, beyond caring if my request to get a table for one came out correctly. She seated me and brought me a glass of water before I could even deliver my carefully rehearsed "*un carafe d'eau.*" I love this place—and Paris is lucky that the afternoon turned out in my favor. I perused the menu, caring little what I ate as long as I ate something. The most appetizing entrée was the *tartes aux tomates avec salade*, which I ordered promptly and ate with no regard to etiquette.

Rested and refreshed from my afternoon snack, I hit the streets once again, this time in search of a market. However, there was not a fruit stand, butcher, or baker to be found behind their glass counters. Evidently markets, like most retail shops, are not open on Mondays. After searching fruitlessly for nearly forty-five minutes, I gave up and headed toward home, my education on courgettes and aubergines, like *l'opticien*, postponed. I was stricken with guilt and worry— soon I'd have to pick up the children from school, and I'd accomplished none of the tasks from the nanny book. I wondered what Estelle would say when she found out. But how could she blame me for the lackadaisical state of Parisian affairs?

But what of dinner? Without the goods from the market, I couldn't very well concoct a salad or quiche for the children. Actually, with my limited cooking ability, it was doubtful I could successfully concoct these items, even with the necessary ingredients, especially when I thought of attempting to operate the state-of-the-art celcius gas oven owned by *les Vladesco*. Once back at the house, I scoured the Vladesco freezer, in which I found all manner of yummy-looking frozen dinners. There was a ratatouille that seemed healthy enough, plus pretty little frozen pizzas topped with rounds of goat cheese and tomato. I decided that for my first night on the job, I would introduce the children to the fascinating world of frozen food gourmet, and write it off as cultural education about a typical American household. I'd have them Americanzed in no time!

By the time I returned to the school gate at 4:15 (pardon—at *seize heure et quinze*) it felt like eons had passed since I had stood there waving good-bye to them that morning. I was exhausted, and I hoped their day had been easier than mine. But as my sweaty little chickadees came rushing through the gates, full of energy, I realized that I'd have to perk up—and fast. Apparently my day had only just begun.

I spotted Léonie first, pushing her way through the swarms of children. Her ponytails were frizzier than ever, poking out from beneath a New York Yankees baseball cap. She ran straight to me with a huge smile, grinning up at me from beneath the shade of her cap. I patted her head and smoothed her ponytails, just as I'd seen her mother do that morning. Then she shyly presented me with a picture she'd drawn. It was hand-colored in a variety of markers, and she'd written in very good English, "Thanks for Keeping Us!" and signed it "Léonie the Star." In a day filled with so many mishaps, her sweet gesture meant the world to me, and I thanked her and pulled her in for a hug.

Next came Constantin, bobbing along amid a dizzying array of six- and seven-year-olds. When he spotted me, he broke from the crowd and ran to greet me with his wide little-boy smile, and immediately began yapping about what *goûter*, or snack, he would "take" when he got home.

"I can go to the park after *goûter*," he said proudly.

Constantin was the only one of the Vladesco children to not have had extensive exposure to the English language. His two older sisters were born in London while Estelle and Alex were still building their finance careers. But Constantin was not born until after the family returned to Paris, and thus was the only member of the family who was not completely bilingual.

In French, the verb *prendre*, "to take," is used as commonly as "I'd like" in American. And though Contsantin did his best to make parallel translations from French to English, his words often came out sounding more like commands than statements. So, instead of saying, "I'd like to go to the park after my snack," the petite monsieur would say, "I can go to the park after my snack." These announcements, combined with his proud-as-a-peacock attitude, made me feel more often than not like he was the boss and I was merely the servant, and I had to train myself to respond as if he had asked a question.

"We'll see, Constantin," I said as he yanked on my arm, running as fast as he could toward home, at least three strides ahead of me the entire way. As I struggled to keep up with him, I couldn't help but laugh. His head bobbed, his limbs failed, and I wondered if he would topple over from the weight of the trunk-size bookbag strapped tightly to his back.

Léonie walked alongside me, not saying a word.

Unlike her brother, she didn't request any special after-school snacks or demand any after-school activities. She merely sighed quietly under the weight of her own book bag. I patted her on the head again and tugged at her book bag, a wordless offer to relieve her of her load. She loosened her arms from the straps and smiled gratefully as her brother skipped ahead.

The minute we stepped into the house, Constantin urged me in the direction of the *goûter* closet. Every day after school, the children were allowed to choose from a closet-full of delicious European cookies and sweets. They were allowed only one sugary selection per day, and choosing a snack was not a task they took lightly. I appreciated their position. If there's anything worth second guessing, it's choosing dessert. Constantin scrambled into the kitchen, scooted a chair up to the counter's edge, climbed onto the chair, swung open the *goûter* closet door, then turned to me with a wide smile, as though expecting praise for his achievement. At the sight of the *goûter assortiment*, Léonie abandoned her adult manners and pensive demeanor, shouting out her request with glee and reminding me that she was just a child, after all.

I glanced at the clock on the wall—just a little after 5 p.m. I expected Diane would appear through the peacock blue doors at any moment though I had no idea how we two would interact. Would she demand her *goûter* as well, or did she abide by a different set of rules? The phone rang, almost as if triggered by my thoughts. I answered it, nervous about conducting a phone conversation in French. But it was Diane.

"Uh, yeah . . . Hi, Rachel, I'm having dinner at a friend's and I won't be home until later. I already checked with my mom, so it's okay," she said. Without waiting for an answer, she hung up.

I hung up the phone with an uneasiness in the pit of my stomach. She hadn't asked me if she could have dinner elsewhere—she told me. And, unlike her brother, I knew enough to know it wasn't an innocent French to English translation.

Despite Constantin's wish to go to *le parc*, I selfishly insisted that we stay home that first night so I could establish some semblance of an evening schedule: *goûter*, homework, baths, dinner, clean up, and finally—bedtime. At this suggestion, Constantin clenched his jaw and crossed his arms tightly across his puffed out chest. I managed to assuage him with the frozen pizza, but I was quickly learning my limits.

My schedule for the evening played out as planned, with a few minor mishaps here and there. While Léonie was polite and obedient, Constantin was proving to be quite a handful. By the time I tucked him into bed at 9 p.m., I was still soaking wet from an earlier struggle with him in the bath-tub. But as I pretended to let him dominate the bedtime story hour by allowing him to choose the story and command me how to read it—"You do the voices"—my worries about his obstinacy quickly faded. I read to him, attempting to coax the little monsieur, who began by sitting upright, arms folded sternly across his chest, into lying down with his head on the pillow. At first it seemed an impossible task, but as the pages turned, he scooted little by little under the covers, and by the end of the story, he was a little darling, curled up with his thumb in his mouth. I knew from Estelle's instructions that she had been trying to break him from this habit, but to me, it was reassuring. He'd gone from dictator to infant in a matter of minutes, and all the hassle of the day, all my ignorance and inadequacy, faded away as he shut his little eyes and went to sleep.

Chapitre Quatre

I'd learned in my high school French class that European business was conducted well into the late hours of the evening, mainly because of a midday hiatus, or siesta, in which lunch plays a vital role. Because I'd fallen into bed exhausted after my first full day as a nanny, the hour at which Estelle and Alex ended their day remained a mystery.

When I found remnants of a dinner for two the next morning, I assumed that hour had been a late one. In the kitchen, roasting pans, vinegar and oil, salt and pepper, and a variety of Alex's preferred *moutardes* were strewn on the stovetop counter. It was still early—not a stir throughout the rest of the Vladesco house—when I slipped through the sliding glass door to collect two dirty plates, two emptied wine glasses, and two soiled white cotton napkins, an elegant leftover display from their evening interlude. I observed the two empty wine glasses stained on the inside rim by a plum-colored film. It was the residue of their table wine. Theirs was that Burgundy beauty raised in the heart of France's Côte d'Or. Alex and Estelle stored at least one hundred bottles of it downstairs in their cellar, all labeled with the name Chanson Père et Fils, Estelle's family wine.

I stood in the garden, which was still gray with the morning haze, mesmerized by the life history of Estelle, who espoused *les Vladesco* to the *anciens riches*. Raised in Beaune, where the heart of Burgundy wine beats a furtive rhythm throughout the historic town ramparts that date to the fifteenth century, Estelle was born to privilege. She grew up the middle of three children in the house of Chanson Père et Fils, a label *depuis* 1750. Nine generations later, Estelle's father owned and operated this gem so treasured by Beaune. The chateau in which they lived was marked a historical monument on the city's map of tourism. The company and all its manicured surroundings belonged to the family, namely Estelle's father, until the late 1990s, when it was tragically sold to some wine and champagne mass-producing conglomerate. I've felt a personal devastation knowing the family sold *Chanson*. Of course it was none of my business, but it broke my heart to know the history, legacy, and tradition had ended.

Estelle left home to go to business school in Paris, where she met Alex. Soon after, they moved to London to pursue careers in finance and banking. But despite her travels and education, I believed the deep red of Burgundy still flowed through her. She exuded an ageless class, bred and fostered like the grapes that grow out of Burgundy soil. No man or measure could extract such a heritage from a person.

Hers was a story like Hermès leather, the way it was first intended for real equestrian accoutrements, before commercialism deflated the stature of an elite class. Aged to per-

fection, smoothed and polished from years of wear and refine-
ment, it was a history of unmatched quality. I longed to know
the original story, and all the characters as they were in their
original setting. But as an observer of her modern life, I saw
that where she had settled was intriguing and beautiful enough.
I walked inside from her garden to her kitchen that resembled
a featured layout in *Architectural Digest*. I rinsed the dirty
dishes clean, careful not to clang crystal and porcelain against
the silver steel base of the sink.

The nanny book sat on the counter where I placed the
glasses upside down to dry. The tasks, compounded with yes-
terday's unfinished ones, had multiplied.

> *Buy pique-nique for journees olympiques—kids may*
> *choose one fruit and one biscuit.*
> *Constantin has judo.*
> *Léonie must practice piano—30 minutes a day.*
> *Diane to the dentiste a 17h30.*
> *Prepare quiche for dinner, yoghurt or fruit dessert.*

Nothing was said about missing *l'opticien*, nor about
the groceries I had not retrieved, but I assumed the note to
prepare the quiche was a subtle hint that frozen pizza dinners
were not encouraged in the Vladesco household. I made a
mental note to spend adequate time testing the workings of
the Celsius gas oven later that day. But first, I wanted to make
a peace offering by having *un rétro* ready and waiting at the
breakfast table, as it should have been on that first day. I still
wasn't certain of the exact definition of *un rétro*, but had figured out by contextual breakfast association that it was some

sort of a bread product. From the aroma that wafted through the open windows, breads—and perhaps *les rétros*—were baking in abundance all across the city. I left the house in search.

I walked the sleepy streets where I discovered a new Paris, one that woke in a cloud of earthy flour. The shuffling feet and whirring car tires and short, blunt horn honks of the day before were gone for the moment, replaced by the doughy aroma of whole grains and rising yeast. I followed the smell and the steady trickle of locals who filed along in the same direction.

I arrived at a bakery with *Le Rétrodor* written on a sign outside. The sign touted several premier awards. Apparently *la meilleure baguette* was a hot commodity and was only sold at a select few *boulangeries. C'est célébré.*

"Une baguette, deux croissants! Trois pains au chocolat!" Inside the *boulangerie*, I discovered a makeshift assembly line of sorts. A serious, ruddy-cheeked woman called out customers' orders to a skinny, nervous-looking girl whose duty was to wrap each pastry and loaf in thin sheets of tissue, then hand the finished product to respective customers. Still a third girl handled the exchange of coins and *centimes*. Every time the ruddy-cheeked woman turned to holler the next order, her ample hips bumped the coin-counter girl from left to right, causing her to drop her change and scramble to pick it up.

"Un pain aux raisins, deux baguettes!" Ruddy Cheeks yelled, throwing her head back for maximum volume. As the line of customers inched forward, I cowered. I was terrified that my French would fail me yet again, ensuring the wrath of

Ruddy Cheeks. I rehearsed *"Un rétro, s'il-vous-plaît"* silently again and again, trying to insert just the right inflection—a nasally punch for the *"un"*; two valiant hockings of air in the back of the throat for the *"rétro."* Only the French considered it an entertaining sport to shove two consecutive guttural "r" sounds into a five-letter word.

I listened to each order, practicing the shape of vowel sounds. Customers uttered consonants and vowels and mouthfuls of sounds from the nose and throat, all stuffed together in one syllable. I mouthed their sounds until it was my turn with Ruddy Cheeks.

"Un rétro, s'il-vous-plaît," I said.

"Un rétro!" Ruddy Cheeks yelled. I wiped the spit from her amplified "r" sounds from where she sprayed my face. With a jerk of her head and a swish of her hips, she gestured me to move aside, which I did, quickly, to let the ruddy-cheeked woman spit in the next customer's face. Following the assembly line, I waited for my tissue-wrapped *rétro* and handed one euro and fifty *centimes* to the coin-counter just in time for Ruddy Cheeks to knock the coins on the floor. A perfect rhythm. Surprisingly, the coin-counter did not seem bothered to spend half her career tossed by the boisterous baker, though for her own sake, I wished she would pick a quiet spot in the corner where managing monetary transactions didn't involve injury.

I left moments later with a loaf of bread that bore a strong resemblance to *une baguette.* By this time the line to Ruddy Cheeks, mostly of housewives on their first of three

Rachel Spencer

daily baguette runs, curved out the door of the bakery and spilled onto the sidewalk.

I walked toward home, famous baguette lodged under one arm the way true French folk carry their bread. The morning sun rose and the flour clouds dispersed, adding a caked layer of sediment to the day-old cigarette butts along the sidewalk's edge. I walked—satisfied, enlivened. It was in this asymmetry, in the blend of cigarette butts and artisan flour, that I first saw into the mystery and history and jazz of the City of Light. Filth and fortune juxtaposed as one. In the bubble of a community I called home, there was no artful engineering. The streets ran straight, one methodically right after the other. The sidewalks stayed swept.

But here, a hundred architectural melodies played at once. There was no congruence, no repetition, no two buildings alike. Yes, it was jazz, the way this city came together. Somehow in the dissonance of art and style and overlapped eras of time, a new song was made. Anything went and everything went, but it was all music. Really good, thoughtful music. And where the sidewalk met the edge of the two iron-barred windows at 37, Boulevard Pereire, I found myself back at home, darting to avoid the street cleaner who stood hosing the cracks of pavement that bordered my basement room windows.

Inside the house that had been still when I left, the espresso machine cranked and churned. Estelle was awake, and busy in the kitchen. I entered, eager to extend to her the carb-packed peace offering.

"Le rétro!" I announced.

She took it. Then she set it aside on the counter. Had I gotten it wrong? I didn't want to ask. So I smiled and accepted the demitasse of inky black espresso she handed me.

"I'll take the kids to school from now on," Estelle said. "I think it's easier that way?" Estelle looked at me over the rim of her demitasse, eyebrows raised, lips curled at the corners, pursed around the edges of her cup.

"Okay," I said.

Clearly she'd used an inquisitive tone for the sake of being polite. It wasn't a question. Had I fallen short on my duties already, or was it truly easier that way? Estelle continued, relaying the day's instructions. She informed me of Diane's whereabouts (she'd already left for school). She gave me directions to the market (there was one nearby open every day of the week—I could have purchased the *courgettes* and *aubergines* after all), and directions to the cheese shop nearby (Alex might ask me to buy cheese occasionally). I smiled and nodded steadily, the only form of communication *en français* I'd mastered thus far.

I tried to keep up with her stream of directions, shops, and instructions. But the more she talked, the more overwhelmed I became. Anyone who's ever traveled internationally understands the term "language barrier." And despite high school and some college French and my best efforts, I remained trapped behind that barrier whenever English was not the primary spoken language. As a result, I was afraid to speak at all. This explains why, even though Estelle spoke fluent English to me, I often remained too timid to speak back with confidence, in any language.

Malheuresement for *moi*, either in French or English, I was seized with such fear and nervousness that I completely lost the ability to form cohesive sentences. To make matters worse, whenever I remembered I was an English speaker, I spoke very slowly, quietly, and with an accent so bizarre even I couldn't figure out to what country I belonged. I called this twist of tongues Franglais. As a result, I wound up sounding like English was my second language. Or my third. Or fourth.

Rather than humiliate myself or cause unnecessary confusion among my new family members, I managed most of my conversations by employing a wide variety of nods and smiles. And occasionally, I threw in a *oui* or a *bon* for friendly measure. After briefing me on the day's agenda, Estelle closed the nanny book and gathered her purse and keys. She left the kitchen and walked toward the front door where I saw Léonie and Constantin waiting, dressed in their school clothes with backpacks strapped on.

"Enjoy Paris," Estelle said. She turned back to me and smiled. Before I could say "*à bientot*," the three were out the door. *À bientot*, I thought. And I was alone in the house again.

I stared at the untouched *rétrodor* on the counter. *Rétrodor*—what a strange name for a dietary staple. It sounded more like a new species of dinosaur than something edible. That, or it was named after some pulverizing bulldozer with which I was not acquainted. It stared back at me, mocked me from its position on the countertop. I thought about devouring it in its entirety. I guessed I *should*, before it embraced its own identity and charged at me across the room on chain-wrapped power wheels. But I resisted, lest a loaf of bread get the best of me first thing in the morning.

I sat at the kitchen table with yet another cup of espresso to reevaluate the nanny tasks of the day. I decided what seemed vital enough to accomplish before noon (nothing) and what I could do in thirty minutes just before picking the kids up from school (everything else). Across the room, the Celsius gas oven mocked me even more boldly than the *rétrodor*. While I didn't foresee the oven sprouting pterodactyl-like wings, and I knew it didn't run on diesel fuel (though Alex would be bloodthirsty for such an oven if it existed), it was far more dangerous than its carb-packed counterpart. A *rétrodor*, I could eat, enjoy, and replace for just 1.50 euros. But if I conducted my own French Cooking for Dummies class and broke the oven in the process, I would have to face the cost of the oven (astronomical) and more severely, the wrath of Alex (immeasurable).

Just as I was reaching for the *rétrodor*, the front door opened. "Ra-chele?" a woman called my name *en français*.

I rounded the doorway of the kitchen and came face to face with a sturdy-figured woman. She was dressed tastefully but plainly and wore large round-rimmed glasses. Her reddish-brown hair, cut short and flat, framed her face. She peered at me expectantly, as if trying to place me, until she broke into a warm smile.

"Maria Celeste!" I exclaimed. *"Bonjour!"* We greeted each other in truest French fashion, kissing first one cheek, then the other.

Maria Celeste was a frisky darling dear of a housekeeper,

who came daily to launder, scrub, mop, iron, dust, and orga-
nize every article belonging to les Vladesco. I'd met her a
couple of years before when I visited Sarah during her nanny
tour of duty. Maria Celeste remembered me mostly because
she loved Sarah and, as later dialogue proved, rated every
nanny since against her—including *moi*.

There was really no reason the house, the laundry, the
linens, the floors, and everything in between needed so much
daily attention; the house was, for the most part, very clean.
But Maria Celeste had a fantastic way of creating catastrophes
out of minor incidents, which typically tripled her workload.
She was originally from Portugal, and spoke rapid French
with what I once called a Spanish accent, though I learned
quickly that such an incorrect geographical reference was
among the highest insults. But Portuguese or Spanish, I
hardly understood a word of it.

We walked into the kitchen and Maria Celeste took
stock of her main chore for the day—the pots and pans Alex
had left on the stove from the previous night's dinner. But instead of gathering the dirty pots and pans and getting to
work, Maria Celeste reached straight for the *rétrodor*, cut a
third of it off, and militantly sliced the rest into one-inch-
thick rounds. As she mumbled something about Alex and his
piggish habits under her breath, she fetched a breadbasket
from the cabinet and placed in it the freshly cut rounds. She
munched the remaining third of the loaf as she inspected a
crusty pan, grumbling.

*   *   *

I spent the bulk of the day musing through town in no partic-ular direction in search of funny French produce fit for heart-healthy dinners. While I wasn't looking forward to concocting an aubergine-filled quiche in the Celsius gas oven, I was quite looking forward to the grocery store outing with the kids to pick up their picnic lunch items for their annual end-of-school field day, or *journées olympiques,* as the French so grandly put it. I arrived a few minutes early to the school gate, anxious for our outing, right on schedule with the nanny book. As I waited, I surveyed the crowd of other nannies and mothers who gathered there, all waiting for their respective competing Olympians. How did they run their households, take care of multiple children, and still manage to look so chic and slim?

My thoughts were interrupted as my own two charged through the school gates. Constantin had mentally planned his shopping spree, and shouted out his list for all to hear be-fore he made it out of the courtyard. "I can take the *saucisson* on *pique-nique!*" he said, obsessed with sausage like the good Frenchman he was. He ran toward me.

"We'll see, Constantin," I said.

"Saucisson! Saucisson!" He chanted, his eyes closed in reverie. Of course I could never let him know how adorable he was, but in my mind, he could take anything his darling heart desired.

Léonie greeted me with her signature girlish grin and more of a twinkle in her eye than usual. She was excited, too, though not as effusive as her younger brother. So we left the schoolyard and set out for the grand Monoprix. I had avoided the Monoprix because it's simply a supermarket like ones we had in the U.S. But walking there with my two Frenchies, I felt like a Frenchie myself. I was just a local, making her necessary trip to the Monoprix after school with the kids. *La vie quotidienne.*

On the way, we dropped book bags at home, and the kids insisted on taking their scooters. Because the sky was looking rather dark, I grabbed an umbrella. I chased Léonie and Constantin the rest of the way to the Monoprix as they raced ahead, and I felt for perhaps the first time like a responsible, loving, reliable nanny. I was shocked and proud at the way I had pulled the day together.

As we walked, the sky grew darker and darker, and a light drizzle started to fall just as we reached the store. Walking the grocery aisles, I hoped all of the customers were equally as fond of *saucisson* as Constantin, who sang the word like an opera baritone. Unlike her brother, Léonie weighed each decision intensely. I understood the seriousness of the matter—this was a rare and special occasion—and let her take her time. She made several trips to and from our shopping basket, returning chosen items back to the shelf and replacing them with better choices. She finally settled on a sandwich of ham and cheese, accompanied by melon and a personal snack-sized box of Lu cookies.

At the checkout, when we gathered our bags—now filled with savory selections of sausage, baguettes, fruit, and personal-sized cookie boxes—I noticed a large group of people standing by the window, peering out. I joined them, careful not to take my eyes off Constantin, who was already prying open his package of sausage. The sky had grown so dark I had to look at my watch to remind myself it wasn't ten o'clock or a later hour. The wind howled and a loud crack of thunder shook the front windows.

Mais oui, the umbrella! I felt a surge of pride run through me, certain I was elevated to greater nanny status with my impeccable precautionary measures. I rushed the kids out the door with their scooters and heard a man yell, *"Bon courage,"* as we stepped onto the sidewalk. I shrugged it off; we lived just a few blocks from the Monoprix. If we hurried, we could beat the worst of it. I snapped open the umbrella. The kids looked up at me with doubtful expressions. I smiled widely, patted their shoulders, and clutched them tighter under the umbrella.

The rain fell in drops, then in stabs, coming down harder with each step. The streets quickly flooded and the wind blew great sheets of water across the ground, making it impossible to discern street from sidewalk. I was used to flooding rains from my lifelong residence in Houston, but this was a serious storm. The kids, I was certain, had never seen anything like it. Léonie stepped from under the umbrella and became our guide, wading bravely through rushing currents. But the water was too high for Constantin. I scooped him up at the waist and carried him, his solid metal scooter, the umbrella, the groceries, and my purse as best I could. Léonie was drenched and I was sick with remorse that I had even considered asking these children to brave such a storm.

We made it home. I fished in my purse for the key, praying it had not spilled out. Got it—whew. I stripped the

Rachel Spencer

kids at the door and left their sopping clothes in a puddle on the front entry steps to start a hot bath upstairs. The phone rang, but I ignored it, unable to deal with the idea of carrying on a conversation in French. Then I saw the kitchen. Water was everywhere. It dripped from the ceiling, where I assumed there were a number of leaks. I turned to the kids and motioned for them to hurry up to the bath. But Léonie, now safe from danger, burst into heaving sobs.

"I want Mommy!" she cried, standing alone in the center of the front entry.

I know, baby, I thought. *I want my mommy, too.*

Before I could comfort her, the phone rang a second time, and for the second time, I ignored it.

I held Léonie and dried the tears from her honest brown eyes. I sent the kids to take their baths, even though it was only six o'clock. I placed buckets under suspected drips in the kitchen, but the rain had mostly subsided. Léonie the Star, living up to her self-proclaimed nickname, padded into the kitchen freshly bathed and in her pajamas, to bring me the mop from Maria Celeste's closet downstairs. I wanted pizza for dinner—and no guilt about it. After surviving the monsoon, the thought of making a quiche was just too much to bear. Afterward we would watch movies in our pajamas until we fell asleep. Movies were pretty much off limits in the Vladesco household, but how could I expect the children to concentrate on their homework after surviving such a traumatic event? Besides, what Estelle and Alex didn't know couldn't hurt them, and I promised myself that I'd get the children back on track the next day with a healthy diet and a lengthy homework session.

Diane came home too, which lifted about thirty pounds of worry from me. She stumbled in, stunned and no doubt freezing, drenched to the bone in a chic, but very see-through, all white ensemble. I prayed silently that she had not been in coed company as she unstuck her thin, cotton shirt from her torso and told me about splashing through the streets with her friends, then racing home. It wasn't until we'd towel dried her hair and she'd changed clothes that I re-membered the nanny book. We missed Diane's dentist ap-pointment. We missed Constantin's judo practice, and we missed Léonie's piano practice. And of all the kids, did I really have to ask Léonie to go upstairs and practice piano? It didn't seem fair. We were all in our pj's in the kitchen, rattling the oven knobs to heat the pizza when I heard a noise at the front door. And then Alex walked in.

Apparently, a neighbor had called him, urging him to rush home and make sure we were okay. She'd called the house several times to check on us, but was worried when no one had answered.

Oops.

Alex had barely even entered the kitchen before asking why the floor was wet. I told him about the leaks, but he looked at me with an almost pitiful glare as if he were sorry I was so stupid.

"Why in the hell didn't you shut the skylight?" Alex said.

"I didn't know how," I said. Did the skylights open?

Until that moment, I had no idea the house even *had* sky-lights. I looked up, but couldn't see anything resembling a normal skylight in the ceiling. And if I couldn't even see the skylights, how could it possibly be my job to know whether they were open or shut? Not to mention, we were caught *in* the storm when the majority of the water poured through the roof. But Alex didn't want an explanation. He pulled out some remote controls from the same drawer that contained the nanny book and house purse. Remote-controlled sky-lights. *Bien sûr*—how foolish of me to not have instinctively assumed *chez Vladesco* came equipped with remote-controlled skylights. He explained how to use them, perturbed that we interrupted his career for such menial tasks. I nodded and smiled in my typical fashion though I wanted to explain that I couldn't possibly have known about the skylights.

Nice, Alex. Really. I'll keep these handy the next time Paris has record-breaking precipitation.

After he left, the kids and I had our dinner and movie time, and I tried to put the whole wretched day out of my mind.

In the words of Scarlett O'Hara, tomorrow was an-other day. And I was more determined than ever to make sure things went smoothly.

The next few days passed without much incident, and I finally felt as though I was adjusting to my routine in the Vladesco household. I was actually quite lonely while the children were away, and in my short time in Paris, I'd grown rather fond of the hour at which I picked them up from school. I arrived early once again, and as I stood waiting on the sidewalk outside the school gate, I resumed the examination I'd begun days before of the many French women around me.

One by one, the slew of nannies and mothers arrived, some pushing strollers, some carrying shopping bags, and some walking alone. I had no way of differentiating mother from nanny—they all looked so young and so French. And they all seemed to know each other. Mingling in the schoolyard was as much a part of their daily routine as anything else. They chatted and generally kept their distance from me. So I stood, friendless and fashionless, on the opposite side of the sidewalk. It was fine with me, though. I was perfectly content staring them straight down to their DNA.

I searched for the gene that made them all so ridiculously thin. No lumps to be found—not a single swollen belly among the group—and I wondered who served as the surrogate mother to all their multiple children?

From the looks of it, I did.

What is it about French breeding? I read *French Women Don't Get Fat* before I came to Paris, in an attempt to morph my mind and body into the French culture. But bestselling book or not, something told me it was way more than a state of mind that allowed these women to pop out one baby after another and still stay thin enough to glide along all smiles in their ballet flats and pleated skirts.

In addition to the thin gene, I also suspected there was a gene for sophistication. It wasn't about matching clothes or color coordinated purses and shoes—it was an overall air of coolness and careless style I just couldn't seem to put my finger on.

There's also a gene for ungreasy hair, which must be somehow connected to the no-sweating gene. Most Parisian women, I'd learned from Estelle, washed their hair a maximum of twice a week. My unruly American hair, on the other hand, became limp and heavy with residue after a mere half day roaming the city streets.

And then there's the mystery of all mysteries—a perkiness gene, *on peut dire,* that allowed the women (mothers!) to go *sans brassière* whenever it suited them.

As I watched them from afar, I re-evaluated my pre-Parisian standards of motherhood. Prior to my trip, my plan for having babies had always been to get really skinny beforehand so I could afford to get fat during and after. But in Paris, the term "baby weight" was seemingly nonexistent. Not only must one remain ridiculously thin after childbirth, but ridiculously trendy as well. Got it. Will do. Even without babies, and despite my efforts at nanny chic, it was obvious I had a lot of work to do on my nanny appearance. Léonie and Constantin never hesitated to let me know when they thought my clothing was inappropriate. One day, when I thought it was okay to run out to the bakery in my sunwashed kelly green cotton capris, Constantin stopped me dead in my tracks at the front door and said something along the lines of, "*No.* Don't wear *that.*" It's amazing how intimidating a seven-year-old fashionista can be.

Léonie was less materially observant, but not less

blunt. One evening after dinner, I asked the kids what they remembered about Sarah and if I reminded them of her.

"You have the same face," Constantin confirmed.

"Except for the nose," Léonie added, pantomiming my nose with a long, sloping motion and a slide trombone sound effect.

"Yeah," Constantin agreed. "It goes like Pinocchio!" He cooed with laughter. I couldn't help but laugh in amazement—the children were more aesthetically astute than I was. *C'est la vie*, I guess.

In those moments, I wondered just how I must have looked to those around me. In America, my J. Crew–laden wardrobe had seemed cute—casual, yet feminine. But whether I was in the Vladesco house, which was filled with Armani and Hermès, or in the schoolyard, surrounded by nannies and moms who looked as though they stepped straight out of the pages of *Vogue*, cute or feminine were far from the appropriate descriptions.

Léonie and Constantin saved me from my pity party, bounding through the school gates swinging their medals and awards from an eventful and hard-earned field day. It was finally the weekend, and just one more school day on Monday.

"Les vacances! Les vacances," all of the school children proclaimed to the sky, to the tree tops, to anyone who would listen. I smiled, remembering the excitement that always came with summer vacation, and ushered my two darlings toward home. For me, summer vacation meant the kids would be home all day, taking my nannying duties from part time to full time. I was just getting used to one schedule, and now I would have

to make yet another adjustment. But I had big plans. I'd saved Le Louvre, Le Musée d'Orsay, shopping at l'Opéra, cruising along the Seine—all the touristy things—to do with the kids. And most pressing, I wanted to take the kids to Notre Dame. It felt like forever since I'd been to church. But ritual and religion aside, it was Notre Dame, for crying out loud. I couldn't wait to take them with me, to a morning mass perhaps, or a vigilant hour of prayer. I knew it would be sacred and something we all would remember forever. But for now, I wanted to go to sleep for the forty-eight hours until that Sunday morning time.

Weekdays in the Vladesco home may have been for working, but the weekends were all about family time. On Friday night, Estelle and Alex arrived home at their earliest hour yet, and Diane even abandoned her busy and very mysterious social life to have dinner with her family. With family time in full swing, I was relieved of my duties and left to unwind after my whirlwind first week on the job. Inspired by the chic school-yard nannies, I donned my favorite pink jacket and new blue jeans—the best attempt I'd made at fashion since my disastrous first day—and set out for an evening walk. I should have been thrilled to have the free time and the gorgeous evening. It was Friday night and I was walking the streets of Paris.

But each time I caught my reflection in the passing shop windows, I looked larger and larger. This was not only due to the lithe French women surrounding me on the streets, but also to the fact that the summer heat was causing me to bloat. My fingers were turning into sausages. That, in combination with my disastrous first week, left me feeling exhausted, irritable, and more than a little homesick. The verdict was in: No matter what country you're in, if your alone, Friday nights are fuel for depression. I just needed a little something to take the edge off, and a therapeutic American romantic comedy was my only hope for salvation and rejuvenation.

And so, on my first free night in the City of Light, I did not visit a museum, or watch the world pass by from a quaint outdoor café. Instead, I headed toward Fnac—a French store best described as an upscale combination of Best Buy and Barnes & Noble. Since I had no girlfriends to gossip with or love interest to pine for, I decided to buy my company for the evening, preferably of the Tom Hanks and Meg Ryan falling-in-love variety. Nothing gives the illusion of comfort and home like a favorite movie.

But when I arrived at Fnac, the building was dark, and I felt a familiar dread settle over me. *It can't be closed! It can't be!* But it was. And thus came my second lesson in Parisian business hours: In addition to being closed on Mondays, local shops and businesses close down early on Fridays. Lovely. Every café was bursting at the seams, but there was no hope for a lonely traveler seeking comfort in electronic media. I turned toward home unaccompanied, discouraged. In the cafés, the tables were dressed up in pristine white tablecloths, and just hearing the laughter and chatter from the dinnertime crowds made me feel swallowed up by my own loneliness. Nearing home, I passed a video rental shop but I didn't have the energy to (1) wait to complete the rental membership and (2) think, speak, and write *en français.*

But then, a few doors down, a sign on the dirty sidewalk

caught my eye. It was a logo I'd cherished on many a lonesome Friday night . . . a sweet, sweet lullaby that had often sung me to sleep.

Ben and Jerry's.

I almost wept with relief. I was saved by my own personal pint of strawberry cheesecake ice cream. Seven euros or not, it was priceless.

I spent the remainder of the evening in the nanny room, listening to the sounds of Friday in the city all around me. With every luscious spoonful, I felt more accompanied until there was no place I wanted to be more than in my bed eating ice cream. I was just drifting away on a cloud of sugary bliss when Estelle poked her head in to tell me she was leaving for her hometown of Beaune tomorrow, and would be back Sunday night late. In the meantime, I would have to watch over Constantin while Alex, Diane, and Léonie were at scuba lessons. Could I do that? Yes, Yes. I made sure to smile and nod in all the right places. She also informed me that Tuesday she and Alex both would be leaving for Normandy for a short vacation. Something about Alex wanting to skydive over the countryside. *Bien sûr.*

The thought of full-time nannying with Estelle and Alex out of reach was not as sweet a reality as my strawberry cheesecake ice cream. But cocooned in my nanny room with the entire weekend ahead of me, Tuesday seemed a billion days away. Besides, I still had half a tub of ice cream left so I decided to forget about it and indulge in the moment.

Bon ouiquend.

Chapitre Cinq

I woke to a small hand petting my face in short, paw-like strokes. When I opened my eyes, Constantin was standing over me with a wide smile, batting his adorable eyelashes. I'd come to recognize this expression as his look of approval, of pleasure, of satisfaction. He was happy with his sleeping nanny. Happy with his Saturday morning.

I grinned back at him and patted the tiny hand cupping my face. I knew by the way the sun beat on the sidewalk and filtered in strong rays through my window that I'd slept until at least mid-morning. The rest of the family was probably already gone, to Beaune and to scuba. From the looks of him, Constantin had not woken long ago, as he was still clad in blue-and-white-striped pajamas, his face still puffy from sleep.

"We can look a film?" he inquired, tilting his head slightly and drawing out the word *film*. He stood, persuading me, affectionately patting my head. He was a flirt, and he'd had enough nannies to know which of his tricks worked the best. How could I possibly say no to such a cherub?

Rachel Spencer

"Good morning, *bébé*," I said. "You want to watch a film? Why don't we have breakfast first, hmm?" I ruffled his messy, slept-on, little-boy hair and led him by the hand out of my room, up the steps, and into the kitchen. I punched buttons on the espresso machine, anxious for its familiar sing-song wake up call. Constantin took his place at the table. He sat upright, his hands clasped astutely in front of him, patiently waiting service as though he were a member of the royal family.

"*Chocolat chaud,*" he said. *Chocolat chaud,* or hot chocolate, was his breakfast of choice and quite simple too for me to make, thank goodness. It was merely Nesquik stirred up with milk and heated in the microwave. Once I'd prepared both our morning brews, we sat together at the table in companionable silence, Constantin happily drinking his *chocolat chaud* while I savored the quietness of the house at mid-morning.

Next, we retreated to my room, indulging ourselves in a film and the laziness of Saturday morning. I picked the film, *My Dog Skip,* and played it in English with no subtitles, much to the dismay of my *petit* boss. After all, he had to learn English somehow, and I couldn't be bothered with reading French subtitles so early in the morning.

We watched until we heard Alex calling down the steps, "Hello-ooo?" His voice was friendly and as full of weekend relief as mine was, and I was glad to greet him upstairs and put the unfortunate skylight incident behind us. He carried several bags, all bursting at the seams.

"You have to see what I bought—it's *fantastique,*" he

said with confidence not unlike his son's, and I wondered at how alike they were. There was something so arrogant, so self-obsessed, and self-assured about Alex that my first instinct was to keep away from him entirely. But there was something more, something in the way he derived great enjoyment from little things, and wanted to share them with others that endeared him to me.

"Have you been to La Grande Épicerie? You have to go," he said, pulling bottles and jars out of the sacs. "Okay, so look at this new sauce—you've never tried anything like it. Okay—*bon*. We have jam . . . some new wine glasses—did you break one last week?" he asked, but his tone was more assuming than inquisitive. I hadn't broken one last week, in fact, he did, but this wasn't the point. He continued showcasing his purchases without looking up for an answer.

"And this is a . . . what do you call it? A nectar. Yes, it's a pear nectar. I mean, it is perfect—the juice from the fruit, you know? *Au naturel*. You have to try it."

He poured some for me and began slicing breads and slathering them with pastes and sauces and compotes for me to try.

"This one you have to try with cheese," he said, wielding yet another jar of jam. Then, out of a different sac that read *Alléosse*, he retrieved several bundles wrapped in wax paper. He sliced a small chunk of stinky, creamy white cheese and poured some of the dark thick jam—black currant, perhaps—on top and held it out to me. "Okay, eat that," he insisted, and I obliged, trying to keep a pleasant smile on my face and chew at the same time.

I'd hardly tasted a thing before he said, "Can you believe it? I mean, it's *fantastique*, right?

"Mmmm. Mpfff," was about all I could get out before he handed me another taste. And another. And another, until we tasted our way through all of his *fantastique* finds. Judging from all of the food spread on the counter, Alex preferred gourmet over scuba. I asked him when the girls would be finished with their lesson.

"Oh please—it's insane," Alex answered. "They do this thing like all day, you know? I don't even know what they do. It's ridiculous." He tossed his head back without one hair of his gelled coif falling out of place. "I'll pick them up in a couple of hours. You want to come?"

I could only imagine him breaching speed limits on the autoroute, daughters in tow, in his brand-new silver Audi A8. He possessed a daring confidence, humorous and sickening at the same time. I couldn't help but laugh.

"I better stay here with Constantin," I replied.

Constantin and I spent the latter half of the day at the *parc*, and we returned home just in time to congratulate Diane and Léonie on passing their scuba tests that morning. They were studying to become trained professional divers in preparation for the family vacation to the Caribbean that December. I was having trouble keeping all of the Vladesco family vacations straight in my head: sailing along the Amalfi coast in August; diving into the Caribbean in December. *Bien sûr.*

Alex double-kissed each daughter on each cheek, then went back to his food, calling out the various items on the dinner menu to everyone in the house and no one in particular. In a few hours, we would dine with Alex's parents, whom the children have lovingly titled Mounie *et* Mip. Mounie is the *grandpère*. Mip, the *grandmère*. It would be one of my first forays into French dining, and I was truly excited for the experience.

The doorbell rang around *dix-huit heures et demi*. I was learning that in Paris, no one ever arrived at the appointed time, but usually a demi of an hour later, at least. In America, this would have been considered fashionably late by some, rude by others. In Paris, it was practically *de rigueur*. I greeted Mounie *et* Mip at the door, and was instantly drawn to their expressive smiles and abundant greetings. They immediately inquired of Sarah, whom they'd met three years ago and loved— of course. We hugged and kissed like old friends, and Mounie kept his arm around my shoulder as we walked up the entry steps and into the living area.

I relieved Mip of the cake she was carrying.

"Un gâteau," she informed me.

"Ah oui," I replied. *"C'est beau! Merci."*

I brought the cake to Alex, who greeted it with a hearty *"Bon!"* and went back to his preparations.

I joined Mounie *et* Mip in the dining room, ready to play hostess. *"Champagne?"* I said, pleased with my pronunciation.

"Bien sûr!" Mounie confirmed for the both of them without hesitation. We would get along just fine. I poured two glasses of bubbly for the guests, and one well-deserved glass for myself.

Mounie began firing questions at me—*en français*—regarding what I did for a living, what my plans were upon returning to the States, where I lived and how I liked it. I took a large sip of champagne for courage and tried, in my most poised French tone, to provide intelligent replies. But these were difficult questions for me to answer in English, let alone French.

The truth was, beyond my tour of duty with the Vladesco family, I had no idea about my plans for the future. I dreaded the thought of going back to the world of office politics and cubicles, not that I even had a job to go back to. I had grad school of course, but I still didn't know if I was even accepted—though I was sure if I emailed my mom, she'd write back to tell me the letter of acceptance had arrived. I sort of left the U.S. banking on getting in, but quite a bit of time had elapsed, and I was starting to get nervous. If I did get accepted (I better have gotten accepted), I needed to register for classes soon. That was probably an important thing to do before, say, August. And yet, it didn't feel especially important. Or urgent. But I was hardly going to admit to Mounie that I wasn't officially a graduate studies student, or that I wasn't sure I even wanted to be. Trying to express those thoughts in French would have just translated poorly, and trying to translate my feelings on the matter in any language was just impossible.

Thankfully, I was saved from elaborating further by Constantin, Léonie, and Diane, who burst into the room at the same time, ecstatic to see their grandparents. During their flurry of greetings, I excused myself to the kitchen to see if Alex needed a sous chef.

"*Bon,*" he said. "You can do the sauce, and if you like, set the table." *Sauce* was his word for salad dressing, but I'd never made it from scratch before, having previously sub-scribed to the bottled dressing school of thought, and I fum-bled with the ingredients, unsure of what to do. Alex sighed in exasperation and took over, mixing together the proper ra-tios of oil, vinegar, and mustard while I stood aside and watched, thinking that if I were able to complete at least one task during my time in Paris without screwing it up, I'd call the entire trip a success.

I was able to set the table without any instruction from the chef, however. The same plates, wineglasses, cheese plates, sets of silverware, and white cloth napkins were used for every meal no matter the occasion. Once I had seven of each arranged, I filled carafes of water and ventured to the cellar, or "cave," as the French call it, for an ample supply of wine. The cave was a room easily as large as the kitchen up-stairs, filled wall to wall with so many bottles of wine I couldn't begin to count. Picking several bottles out of such an impres-sive collection was harder than I thought, but it was the one detail Alex was fairly lax on.

"They're all *fantastique*, okay? Just pick a few," he had hollered at me as I left the kitchen to begin the search as he instructed. Most of them were from Chanson, but I was feeling adventurous, so I choose three bottles from Bordeaux instead.

"*Bon,*" Alex noted in approval of my selection. Then

Rachel Spencer

he called out, *"À table,"* and beckoned all of us to the table to commence the feast.

We began with a first course of grilled chicken skewers coated in a savory peanut sauce while Alex grilled his rack of lamb. I stood to retrieve the salad and sauce from the kitchen until I remembered that in French dining, the salad is the last course.

The meal was long, leisurely, and delicious—one of the best of my life. Alex's menu was simple, yet utterly fulfilling: medium rare grilled lamb, carrots roasted with olive oil and sea salt, thinly sliced cucumbers tossed in vinegar and sunflower oil, and rounds of crusty French bread. All throughout dinner, the conversation was warm and pleasant, and I felt myself grow more and more relaxed with each new course, each sip of wine. The kids begged for tastes of wine every few minutes, and Alex regaled us with stories of growing up in Romania, and how their small family fled to France when he was fifteen to escape the Communists. He talked of how they had nothing save for the clothes on their backs, and of the hardships Mounie *et* Mip endured in order to take care of their family. The conversation gave me an entirely new respect for Alex. Suddenly his sense of entitlement and self-congratulation made more sense. His life was the product of hard-earned success, and he did not waste a moment of it. He enjoyed both work and play, and throughout the course of the evening, he embraced his children just as often as he picked up his glass of wine.

When Alex finally served the green leaf salad at the

end of the meal, he insisted that I had prepared the dressing. I started to protest, then stopped myself. My first week on the job had taught me never to argue with Alex, especially when it came to food. So I gratefully accepted the credit.

As the sleepy children filed off to bed, he beckoned to Diane to bring the cheese plate and the espresso. She did so without any fuss or complaint, surprising me with her obedience. Even though she had matured quite a bit in the few years since I'd last seen her, around her parents, Diane was young, innocent, and respectful. Alex served the cheese, explaining each type, where it originated, how it was prepared, and how the cheese shop owner favored him over all the other customers.

I nibbled my cheese and sipped my espresso, wondering at this family, with all of their history, all of their stories, all of their adventures and triumphs and disappointments. And I wondered what types of stories I would tell my own family someday. Surely my trip to Paris would be among them—but what would I tell? How would it end? I didn't speak. I just ate my stinky cheese, sipped my espresso, laughed when they laughed, and stared into the black sky that had become the warm Paris night.

On Monday, Alex and Estelle left for their trip to Normandy. And on Tuesday, the first official day of summer vacation, the nanny book was beautifully empty. Though school was out for the little ones, Diane still had end of school exams, and was staying with a friend while she finished them. Even though I was looking forward to spending quality time with her once school was out, I was greatly relieved not to be responsible for her while her parents were away.

Léonie and Constantin, on the other hand, were free from all care and the most elated I'd ever seen them.

I knew just the way to commence the season of leisurely indulgence and had no trouble convincing the kids to join me for a trip to the premier *rétro* spot in town. I rounded the children up, got them dressed, and we headed out into the warm Parisian morning and toward the best bakery in the city. It won *premier* in various awards year after year, and not just for the bread. I wondered why it wasn't bigger or more commercialized, but that's the wonderful thing about Paris—you don't have to be big and commercialized to be good or famous. In fact, if you are big and commercialized, you're probably not nearly as good as the humble places. When we arrived at the bakery, which was completely nameless to the passing pedestrian except for the lettering that read *"Boulangerie-Patisserie"* on the window, I felt my stomach rumble. Despite my daily cravings, I had partaken only minimally in the buttery bakery delights available on every street corner. This was partly due to my new espresso diet, which curbed all of my cravings, and partly due to the sheer stress of getting through my days without any major catastrophes.

By the time we got to the front of the line, my appetite was in full swing, birthing a gastronomical love affair between me and the rows of pain au chocolat lining the glass case. Léonie and Constantin ordered *pepites*, a chocolate chip–speckled sweet bread that was enormous in size. It deceived tourists like me into believing one could eat it and stay as fit as the rest of the skinny Parisians standing in line. But I had a secret suspicion that every Parisian buying pastries was really buying them to feed to their fat American houseguests. Léonie and Constantin didn't quite count in my case study because their little metabolisms were still too young to be affected by the evil of fats and sugars. Once I got the two *petits* settled down with their two *pepites*, I watched them turn from civilized little Frenchies to rudimentary rugrats with chocolate-smeared mouths while I devoured my *pain au chocolat* with frightening speed.

I was still smiling when Léonie looked at me and said, "Did you already finish yours?"

"Oh, I guess I have," I said, licking my fingers shamelessly.

"Hmm," she said, turning back into a civilized Frenchie. "I like to *enjoy* mine."

Great. Mere hours into summer vacation, and already my behavior was being tallied and marked by an 11-year-old girl. So much for relaxing. I wanted to tell Léonie my pastry was like half the size of hers but I realized if I did I would (a) be arguing with an eleven-year-old about my diet, and (b) remain unjustified because despite her pastry being larger, her rear end was not just half the size of mine, but one-fourth at most.

I felt the sudden need to return to the miracle-working espresso machine at the house, but instead coerced the kids into a long walk, as much to keep them amused as to burn off the bakery calories. So on we walked. I already sported a grease spot on my shirt as evidence of my love affair with the pastry, Léonie boasted her pint-sized *derriere*, and Constantin smacked his lips together as indication that he'd found his breakfast pleasurable.

Surviving the streets in Paris was a medal-worthy accomplishment, especially for a girl who is used to tooling around the Houston suburbs in a car. When braving the streets alone, I was always a little nervous getting from one crosswalk to the next. When I added Léonie, who often bolted ahead to prove her independence, and Constantin, who liked to stop in between passing cars for a smile or conversation, I was downright terrified. So my maternal instincts kicked in and I took to yelling, *"Attention! Faites attention!!"* every time we neared a crosswalk and grabbing Constantin's hand if not scooping him up altogether before stepping out into the crazy madness that is Paris traffic. I wondered if they offered classes in *off*ensive driving, particularly around l'Étoile, rather than the defensive driving that is proactively taught in the U.S. Although driving in Paris was probably quite a rush, just getting the two children safely through the streets was enough to satisfy the thrill seeker in me.

As we walked, we made our way around the *place* toward Avenue Niel, my route of choice for daily produce shopping, and also the street that turns to Avenue MacMahon, one of the twelve vessels leading out from l'Étoile at l'Arc de Triomphe. The produce stands occupied most of the alleys between the marketplace streets. Bins of fresh apricots, plums, and kiwis formed a wall of fruit separating one stand from the next. Tables piled with cantaloupe and mango lined the edges of the street. Buckets and baskets of fresh strawberries and raspberries, of a size and beauty the likes of which I had never seen before were artfully arranged in between large displays of melon. The vegetable stands intermingled with the fruit stands, piled with products like my old friends courgettes and aubergines, as well as myriad cabbages, lettuces, and greens.

We walked down the aisles from one stand to the next, sniffing for the best choices. The locals hand-selected every item, squeezing to verify ripeness, proper texture, ample juice, and all-around best in show. In America this would be considered rude; in France the farmers stood by prospective buyers with great pride, waiting for approval of their display. If the prospective buyer did not award the farmer's stock a passing grade, the farmer would then join in the search, performing squeeze, sniff, and even taste tests of his own until he sent the customer away as if they were old friends with not one but two bushels of whatever item had undergone scrutiny.

As we rounded a corner, a distinctive, unpleasant odor overpowered the lingering sweetness of fresh fruit and earthy vegetable goodness. I couldn't place it right away, though the smell was familiar. Constantin, ever the proper Frenchman, lifted his head in alert and led us to a storefront a few steps away. When I saw the name Alleosse printed across the awning, the same as the logo on the bags from Alex's Saturday shopping trip, I knew cheese was inside. Constantin and Léonie tugged me inside, eager to survey the shop's daily offering of fromage. Near the entrance of the tiny shop was a solid wheel of cheese so large that Constantin could have laid down on top of it with room to spare. Léonie made her way to the counter, looking lustfully at the *crottins de chèvre*, some rolled in herbs, some encrusted in ash. I spoiled the kids, and myself, with a small taste of creamy white *crottins*. But the chèvre seemed only to heighten our appetites, and by the time noon rolled around, we'd visited at least a dozen more stalls and the kids were whining for lunch.

For a lunch out and about in Paris, there is nothing better than a baguette and a *poulet rôti* to share among friends or, in my case, *petit* friends. Do not confuse the *poulet rôti en baguette* with its rather boring English translation: roast chicken on bread. Buying a *poulet rôti* hot off the streets from one of the many Parisian rotisserie stands is no minor league experience. Order one *coupé*, and the games begin.

But since I was an American in Paris, I was unfamiliar with the street fare and its serving rituals. I was among the tourists who thought by ordering *"Un poulet rôti, s'il-vous-plaît,"* I would walk away with a neatly boxed chicken and perhaps some plastic cutlery, as it is *très populaire* to take lunch in the style *pique-nique*.

Ah, I still had a lot to learn.

When I gave my order to the friendly rotisserie man, he replied, *"Coupé?"* and then nodded at the children for encouragement. Rather than stop to think about the meaning of the word before replying, I nodded and smiled out of habit and said, *"Bien sûr!"* before I could stop myself. Then I flipped through my mental French to English dictionary as quickly as I could.

Coupé, coupé . . . The meaning of the word didn't dawn on me until the rotisserie man pulled out a set of crazy-looking chef's knives. Of course! *Coupé* meant "to cut." With a *"Bon!"* and a grunt, the rotisserie man—we'll call him Monsieur Rôti—chose a *poulet*, cooked to a luscious golden brown, and sent it flying. I stood in wonder as Monsieur Rôti threw the chicken into the air, caught it on the tip of one knife, and batted it back into the air with the other knife. Without deviating from his task, Monsieur Rôti winked and nodded at us, as if already expecting applause. But his teasing look said, "Oh wait—there's more," and off he went once again with the knives.

Monsieur Rôti chopped with devilish delight, slicing every last bit of the succulent meat from the bone. The blades of his knives glistened with juices as they flew side to side to side. Then with one swipe of the blade, Monsieur Rôti cleared the surface of his chopping block, sweeping our meat into a sac and tossing the carcass and scraps to the dirty sidewalk below. I looked down at the filthy street in surprise, wondering what beggar or dog had first dibs on Monsieur Rôti's scraps.

Monsieur Rôti presented me with a tied plastic bag containing every ounce of meat from the once-whole *poulet*. *Coupé. C'est magique.* I walked away in amazement, leaving Monsieur Rôti to his long line of waiting customers. The whole scene amused me more than it did the children, as this was an ordinary occurrence to them.

Perhaps the most marvelous thing about eating a *poulet rôti coupé* on fresh baguette is that the steam and fresh juices from the meat make enough moisture to create their own sauce. By simply cutting the baguette and stuffing the middle full of meat, the two components stick together perfectly to form *un sandwich extraordinaire*. Even the most prim of my civilized Frenchies approved of this gourmet meal. We stuffed the baguette with the hot *poulet*, tearing it in hunks to gobble. Breaking bread together, we munched happily in silence and left not a bite unsavored. Afterward, I took turns carrying Léonie and Constantin on my back as we walked the mile or so home, partly because their little legs had walked far enough for one day, and partly because I wanted to make sure our entire outing and their entire prelude to *les vacances* was grandly entertaining.

The day was going far too well to be over. Not long after we returned home, the phone rang. I ran for it, assuming it was Diane calling to check in.

"Hello, Rachel?" It was Estelle.

"Yes—hi!" I said, raising my voice above the friendly din of the house. Constantin was occupied using one of my legs as his personal jungle gym while he sang a song about *l'escargot* at the top of his lungs. Léonie had turned on the stereo full blast and danced around us to the wild melody of Abba's "Dancing Queen."

"Did Léonie attend her piano rehearsal?"

I didn't answer, mostly because I had no clue what she was talking about, and I was certain Estelle would not be impressed if I asked her to clarify. I flipped frantically through the nanny book, sure that it was empty. But in my panic, I couldn't find the correct page. I had already checked it that morning! The first day of *vacances* and the nanny book was empty, right? On the other end of the phone, Estelle sighed impatiently.

"Um, no," I finally answered, while attempting to unpry Constantin from my leg, turn down the stereo, and be as professional as possible. I continued flipping pages for notes on a rehearsal.

"Hmm." There was a long pause. Estelle was very skilled at delivering the most intimidating long pauses. I had the distinct impression that, if she were standing in the room with me, the corners of her mouth would be turned up in a wry smile.

"This is very disappointing," she said in a tone I didn't recognize from her. Whatever the tone, it was rather clear that Estelle was not amused. Then she switched to French, which she rarely did with me, knowing full well I could not understand what she was saying. Thank heavens, because I couldn't stand the heat.

When she finally switched back to English, she instructed me to rush immediately to the house of the Baroness, where the rehearsals were held. I hadn't the slightest idea of the Baroness's address, or how on earth I would find my way there, but I didn't dare ask. Instead, I prayed silently that Léonie would know the way. I wanted to say something to Estelle, to apologize, to offer some sort of consolation so she would believe I was taking good care of her children while she was away. But from her tone, I knew I had committed too grave a fault to even make an apology worthwhile. Instead, I swallowed my words and hung up the phone with no more than a serious "thank you" that was full of remorse, apology, and immediate repentance.

After I hung up, I stood staring at the date in the

nanny book. I must have looked at the wrong page that morning. There was a long list of items—food to buy at the market, pants to take to the tailor's, Diane's end of year exam schedule. And right in the middle of it all, at twelve noon exactly:

Repetition—Léonie, 17, Boulevard Malesherbes

Répétition means "rehearsal." A piano rehearsal, in this case.

With no explanation, I swooped up the kids and raced out the front door with Estelle's words ringing through my head. Disappointing. Ugh.

Léonie immediately realized the problem and became very serious, like she was channeling the frustration of her mother. Léonie was a dutiful, focused child who took a very vigilant approach to her schoolwork and her extracurricular endeavors, with very little adult supervision. I'd not once asked her to practice her piano, yet she did so every day, willingly. I often heard her upstairs, pounding away on intermediate level Bach while Constantin and I played games and puzzles and cards. Knowing how dedicated she was to her practice made me feel even worse about missing the rehearsal.

Much to my relief, Léonie knew the way to the Baroness's. We arrived more than two hours late at a grandiose townhouse, and Léonie anxiously rang the bell while I stood behind like an ill-behaved puppy. Despite our late arrival, Léonie was allowed a delayed practice. Constantin and I waited outside, and passed the time by taking a walk down the street. When I retrieved her from her lesson, I also learned of her recital, which would be held in the Baroness's home in just a few days' time.

I spent the evening, after supper and bedtimes, carefully outlining my responsibilities for the following day, determined to fulfill all of them. Diane would be finished with her exams by then, and she had three free days before heading to Spain for an exchange program. I was hoping to spend some quality girl time with her as well. After nearly two weeks in the sole company of children, I was ready for a little bit of teenage energy. But the truth was, in the entire time I'd been living at the Vladesco home, I'd hardly seen Diane at all.

Chapitre Six

In addition to the fact that I was failing daily to fulfill my nanny duties, Diane was beginning to weigh more heavily on my mind. Her mysterious absences had become a constant source of worry in the pit of my stomach, despite Estelle's assurances to the contrary that everything was fine.

Despite our warm greeting on my first day, Diane had breezed in and out of the house with little regard to me the handful of times I'd seen her since. However, considering the fact that I was still adjusting to my new nannying duties, and considering she often took dinner with friends (with her mother's permission), I had no reason to believe there were any real problems than a Constantin-size handful. At fourteen, Diane was probably too old to need a nanny. But I figured at the very least we could be friends—we could go on lunches and go shopping or maybe even see a movie.

My Pollyanna daydreams came to a shattering end the afternoon I expected her home from her last exam. Léonie was playing at a friend's house and I had just dropped Constantin off at his two-hour pottery class. I spent the entire walk home planning a shopping trip with Diane, as now seemed the perfect time to venture out together. I turned my key in the door the three times around it requires to unlock, unlock again, then unbolt the door, and pushed the door open to what I thought would be an empty house.

But no. Instead, I heard male voices, teenage male voices, and I looked up and found myself face to face with five teenage boys. Now, I didn't even know what to do with teenage boys when I was a teenager, and the sad truth was, I hadn't made much progress since then.

They stood in the entryway to the kitchen, and, strangely enough, they looked like they had been expecting me, though I'm sure they were just as surprised to see me as I was to see them. I instantly felt the need to hold up a NO LOITERING sign as if they had intruded after hours in a public park. But I knew better. They were in the house because they had been invited into the house. By Diane.

I wanted to ask them who they were, but instead I said nothing and breezed past them on into the kitchen, which was easily full of as many girls as boys. I was seized with panic and unsure of what to do. I *did* know there were way too many teenagers in the kitchen, though. Estelle specified that Diane was to have no more than two female friends over at one time. She'd never mentioned a rule about male friends, probably because they weren't supposed to be there at all. A reasonable rule for a fourteen year old, but obviously one that Diane found debatable.

I stared at Diane without saying a word, giving her

ample time to offer up an explanation or apology. But she did neither. She just stared back at me as if she was perturbed I'd interrupted her party at all.

"Umm . . . Diane?" I said, trying to give her another opening in which to explain herself.

"Uhh, yeah, we're just leaving," she said with such blasé nonchalance I was almost convinced that it was appropriate for her to set the rules. At her words, her group gathered up their things. I was absolutely boiling with anger. She *knew*. She *knew* she wasn't supposed to be there and she *knew* she could take advantage of me. Well, I wasn't going to let that happen. I wanted to seem strong and sure, like a respectable authority. But when I opened my mouth to speak, the familiar and frustrating language block took over, and my voice came out small and weak. "Ooo-okay," I said in my strange Franglais accent, and stood back, feeling helpless, as Diane and her crowd filed out of the house, unhindered and entirely unaffected by my presence, lest it be unclear who held the reigns. As angry as I was at her disobedience, and even though I had no idea where she'd gone to, it was okay that she left. Spending the afternoon supervising a houseful of hormones high on summer fever was a job that even I, failing nanny as I was, didn't deserve. Whether she was allowed to be leaving the house again or not, I was relieved to dismiss Diane and her caravan from my supervision.

Once the walls had stopped vibrating, I ventured into the kitchen to commence a thorough investigation of whatever youthful activity I had interrupted. On the counter over the bar cabinet was an open bottle of *rhum*. On another counter, the disassembled parts of a blender lay in small puddles of juice. The sink was filled with juicy film-lined glasses, which had obviously contained whatever my little chef had prepared for her guests. I sniffed one of the glasses. Whatever they were drinking, it was definitely alcoholic. Now, I know that the legal drinking age in Europe is under twenty-one, but I'm pretty sure it's not as young as fourteen.

I quickly put the *rhum* away and washed the dishes, hoping to have the place spic and span before Maria Celeste arrived. That woman was a detective for trouble and a mess as *très grave* as this one would be sure to set off her sirens, especially where Diane was concerned. She threatened to quit almost every time we talked about Diane, impressing upon me the importance of taking action at her behavior.

"C'est PAS bon!" she always said, with a dedicated emphasis on the *"pas."*

To which I would reply something along the lines of *"Ahh oui! C'est pas bon! Elle écoute pas?! Non!"* I agreed with Maria Celeste that indeed, Diane didn't listen, and no, the situation was not good. But despite her concerns being valid ones, Maria Celeste and my mock responses provided me more comic relief than cause for concern.

Even though I couldn't really understand Maria C, I was smart enough to know that the conversations were *très* important to my relationship with her. I wanted her to know we were working toward the same goal. Besides, Maria C loved to tell stories of the poor jobs previous nannies had done (except for Sarah, of course). And though I knew I would never be elevated to Sarah's angelic heights in Maria

C's mind, I didn't want to be lumped into the "bad nanny" category, either.

To keep Maria C from growing an ulcer, I dried every glass and returned it to its proper place. I realized this was the worst thing I could do if I wanted Diane to understand the consequences of her actions, but I didn't have the backbone to nag her to clean up her own mess, let alone facilitate the therapy sessions that obviously needed to take place here. After all, I was just the au pair and since Estelle gave Diane all the freedom in the world, what could I really do about it? Realistically, my authority as an au pair meant about as much to Diane as Maria C's squawking French meant to me.

Because Estelle and Alex were away for the next two days, I feared Diane's rather rebellious independence would continue unhindered. However, Diane was supposed to sleep at home tonight, and I would have a talk with her. Ignoring the knot of fear that had lodged in my stomach, I went about my afternoon duties with the younger children while mentally rehearsing what I would say to Diane when she came home. I also mentally rehearsed what I would say to Estelle upon her return. It would be tough, but I felt I could endure the next two days knowing that authority would soon be enforced.

But by dinnertime, Diane was still not home. I set the table for four anyway in hopeful anticipation, though quite frankly I wanted her home more for my own relief than because I was in any way looking forward to our next encounter.

"À table!" Constantin screamed up the stairs to Léonie, who was perpetually attached to the computer on the fourth floor, frantically instant messaging her friends. If she weren't

so instantly obedient, I would have tried harder to pry her away from her cyber social life.

Constantin waited a mere thirty seconds before again summoning his sister to dinner. *"À table!"* he screamed in a voice so shrill I cringed while filling our tableside water decanters. Still, I couldn't help but smile at his antics. Though Constantin was rarely instantly obedient himself, he demanded an immediate response from everyone around him, or at least their immediate attention. Yelling the phrase that beckoned the family to the table at meal time provided a sense of accomplishment for his ever-growing ego and his burgeoning man-of-the-house status.

Just as we were sitting down to dinner and I was exhaling for maybe the second time all day, the phone rang.

"Allo?" I answered, trying to sound as French as possible.

"Uhh, yeah. Hi, Rachel, it's Diane." She paused for a moment, and I thought I heard giggling voices in the background. "Yeah, I'm having dinner with friends. I'll be home later."

"Uhhh . . ." I stammered, knowing I should interject or protest here, but my mind was completely blank, and Diane hurried on before I could think of something to say.

"I called my mom, she said it was fine, okay? 'Bye." The dial tone blared in my ear. It was the second time that day Diane had blatantly ignored me, and I was starting to believe I had lost all ability to formulate opinions or make decisions.

I hung up the phone and returned to the table, where Léonie and Constantin were looking at me expectantly. I gave them what I hoped was a reassuring smile, then I collected Diane's empty place setting and put it away quickly before my inability to take charge could be questioned by the younger souls staring up at me.

The rest of the evening passed with no sign of Diane, but without incident. After dinner, Léonie went back to cyberspace and Constantin amused himself by my side, while I straightened up the kitchen and prepared for the next day. I was just prying Léonie away from the computer and into bed at 9:30 when I heard the door downstairs slam, followed by footsteps in the foyer. Knowing Diane was home and safe and out of trouble made it instantly easier for me to get the other two to sleep.

Before retiring to my nanny room, I called, "Good night," through Diane's shut bedroom door. As long as she was on the other side, I was completely content going to bed with no other exchange of words. Confrontation was never my strong suit, but the peace allowed me to continue sanely in the nanny role for now.

"Good night," she replied. Her tone was friendly, even sweet. Perhaps I had overreacted and things would be okay after all. I smiled, having received enough of a dosage of peace to get me through the night.

I woke up earlier than usual the next morning, probably because I'd actually rested for the first time since I'd arrived. I sat in the kitchen hovering over my morning espresso, grateful to have a few more moments to enjoy it than usual. I loved this new obsession. It was my constant—the only thing I had with me from the beginning, unchanging. Plus, I was convinced I really was losing weight through its charms and my dedication to it, so this made me an even bigger fan of, if not a slave to, my morning ritual.

I was at the end of the kitchen table, savoring my brew, when I heard footsteps coming down the stairs—big footsteps that certainly were not the darling pitter-patter of Léonie and Constantin. Considering the only other possibility, I assumed investigation mode, turning immediately from espresso-lover to detective agent. From my vantage point at the table, I could see the foot of the stairs, the entryway, and the front door. I repositioned myself slightly so as to appear oblivious to the action, yet through my peripheral vision, I had keenly activated my spy radar.

There was some muffled laughter, then as suspected, Diane crept into view. She moved cautiously, holding her hand behind her to lead someone. I listened for another voice, but heard nothing. Then the mystery person came into full view—a boy. Diane was leading a boy down the stairs and to the front door. *Incroyable!* It was all I could do to not whip my head to the right and stare him down. As soon as they turned their backs I slyly adjusted my head and watched in horror. They paused at the front door, her hand resting on his chest. He took her other hand in his, swinging it playfully. I listened to an exchange of way-too-adult-sounding good-byes followed by a casual kiss on the lips. You know, the kind you do without thinking because it's such a familiar habit.

Now, I'm not going to deny kissing before I was fourteen, but I certainly didn't have it down the way she did. The art of the morning-after farewell hardly made sense to me in the movies, let alone in real life. Who *was* this girl?!

As she turned away from the door, I forgot all about playing detective. I stared at her openly, my mouth agape. She sauntered blithely up the steps, caught my gaze, and said, "Good morning," without hesitation or remorse. Then she pursed her lips, smiled at me, turned, and continued up the stairs. It wasn't a sweet smile or a befriending smile. It was the kind that says *I'll show you*—the kind that only a woman can execute. But she was not a woman. And I was certain that even if fourteen was the legal drinking age, fourteen was definitely too young to own that look. She owned it, though, and threw at it me with a cunning and effortless toss.

Shit.

Now, I don't like to cuss. It's not ladylike, it's not commendable, and there are better ways to express a point. But at that given moment, all other words evaded me. I didn't say it loud—I didn't actually say it at all. I just thought it. And thought it. And thought it. And thought it.

By the time Estelle and Alex returned home the next night, my original rehearsed conversation with Estelle had now grown from *une petite probleme* to *un grand catastrophe*.

I was downstairs in my room when I heard the front door slam. I paced back and forth, debating whether to bring it up tonight or leave it until the morning. On one hand, I hated to go one more day of allowing Diane free rein, on the other, I was tired and I dreaded giving Estelle the report. I was still pacing when Estelle called my name through the door. I eyed the windows for an escape route, but gave up upon realizing that my head would have gotten stuck in between the iron bars outside. Facing my fear, I opened my bedroom door.

"Hi, did you have a good trip?" I asked in a perky tone, avoiding the inevitable. Estelle entered the room, and I, restraining from pacing, stood as still as I could manage.

"We did. How were the kids?" Estelle was never one to delay a meeting's agenda.

"They were good!" I said, straining to keep the perky tone. "Or fine, rather," I corrected. "Umm, actually, I need to talk about something," I answered at last, leaving both of us uncertain of what expression to hold on our faces.

Estelle narrowed her eyes in suspicion and cocked her head to one side, listening. I wondered if she knew already. But how could she? I wouldn't put it past Maria Celeste to get all up in arms and call the *madame,* but I was pretty sure even Maria Celeste was clueless about the events. Keeping my voice calm and even, I told her about the *rhum* incident.

"You saw her drinking?" Estelle questioned, wrapping her confident composure around her like a trenchcoat. Now someone else was playing detective and I was in the plaintiff's chair. *No, I didn't see her drinking*, I wanted to say, *but does it matter? I mean, I saw evidence everywhere and the point is, she's fourteen!*

"No, I didn't see anything. I came into the kitchen as she and her friends were leaving and I saw everything out after she had already left."

"Where were they going?" It was a totally logical question, yet until now, it hadn't occurred to me.

"Umm . . . I didn't ask," I responded, explaining that with all the friends she had over who shouldn't have been there in the first place, she'd left me stunned. As I spoke, I realized I was sounding more and more to blame here. My primary responsibility is to know where the kids are at all times. I didn't. I had messed up. I felt myself shrinking, as if sliding from the plaintiff's chair would relieve me of accusation.

"Hmm," Estelle murmured, no longer trying to hide her irritation. I had yet to master reading Estelle's many expressions, but I had every reason to believe this irritation was directed not at her unruly daughter, but at the very irresponsible nanny standing in front of her. I had to defend myself—I was, after all, the only one available to plead my case.

"I know this doesn't look good on my part, but there's something else I need to tell you." Estelle stood still, readily accepting my further plea. "The next morning, when I was up in the kitchen, I saw Diane walk a boy out of the house."

Estelle maintained her calm stance, her face unaffected.

"Did you see him come in that morning?" Estelle asked.

"Umm, it was early. I'm pretty sure he was leaving from the night before," I answered.

"You are sure he didn't come that morning?" The thing is, I really wasn't sure. I didn't see him come into the house. But the smile on Diane's face after the boy left had told me everything I needed to know. And I wasn't about to leave myself open to blame just because Estelle couldn't see the truth about her daughter.

"Yes," I answered, looking her straight in the eye. At this revelation, Estelle's eyes widened considerably.

Estelle looked at me for several long moments, her lips curling into the disappointed, wry smile I was getting to know very well.

"Hmmm," Estelle thought out loud. "I'm going to have to have a serious talk with her," she said, brushing off her pants legs as if to wipe the episode from her mind.

That's it? I thought, as she turned to leave the room. I don't know what I was hoping for, but I had an uneasy feeling that things weren't going to be resolved as easily as I had at first thought. So Estelle was going to have a talk with Diane. Great. But when? And what was *I* supposed to do in the meantime?

"Should I say anything to Diane?" I asked, half hoping she would say yes, half hoping she would say no.

"No, I will—soon," she said. "Good night."

And that was that. After worrying myself sick, the only solution I got from Estelle was *wait*. I was sick of waiting. I hated waiting. Especially when I didn't know what I was waiting for.

Chapitre Sept

Thursday morning. It was two days and counting until Diane left for Spain. The maternal part of me still wanted to reach out to her before she flew off to a foreign country. But the frustrated nanny part of me left her unattended, sleeping in her room while I took the lower maintenance kids to the *parc*, where I ran off my frustrations in healthy form by chasing Léonie and Constantin as they swirled around on their scooters.

A late-morning drizzle caused us to retire from scooter-chasing activities early—a grave disappointment to the children, who were inflicted with summer fever. I promised the sunshine-hungry little ones that we would watch a movie at home and make the most of the rainy day. Movies and television were against the rules, but I saw nothing wrong with spoiling the children royally every once in a while. It made them happy, and if they were happy, then I figured I could write off my nannying duties as a job well done.

As we made our way home, Léonie raced ahead of her brother and me, then rode back and forth down the street until we caught up to her.

Once there, Léonie begged me for the key to unlock the door, a favorite task of hers. Since the *rhum* episode, a twinge of anxiety crept up in me every time the key hit the front door. But following the kids into the house, I saw that everything was quiet and relatively clean, save for a pile of pink, silk-flowered corduroy blazers piled on the entryway floor. I smiled in relief. Girls upstairs in Diane's bedroom was heaven compared to the catastrophes I had imagined while walking home. I could deal with coats lying around. I was *happy* to deal with coats lying around. I sent the little ones down to my bedroom to pick out *un film.* *"En Anglais!"* I cried out to them, knowing if they were going to rot their brains with television, at least they would do so while perhaps sharpening their English, a skill I'm supposed to regularly enforce.

Knowing that Diane was under control and the kids were happy, I turned my attention to the more important matter of food. I was getting more comfortable in my environment, and with the Celsius stove. Plus, I'd finally figured out what aubergines and courgettes were (eggplant and zucchini), and I was anxious to put them to use.

I was also inspired by Alex's culinary escapades. My favorite thing about Alex's cooking was his inconsistency, which to me was the sign of a true artist. No meal was repeated, no menu was imitated. Alex had mentioned several times that ratatouille was *très facile* to make from scratch, and in the Vladesco family kitchen on a rainy afternoon with so many fresh vegetables on hand, ratatouille seemed the perfect lunchtime choice. I pulled out the aubergines and munched some leftover *rétrodor* as I chopped, eager to soak the bread rounds into the hot stew.

Aubergines, courgettes, tomates, carottes, squash (which was also called *courgette*, I believed*), un petit d'oignon, et garlique, bien sûr*, I sang to myself as I assembled the ingredients. I was happily chopping away when I heard footsteps and voices coming down the stairs. I cowered, my healthy appetite retreating at the thought of dealing with Diane and company. I tried to think of something to say as they entered the kitchen, but my language capabilities had, naturally, suddenly gone the way of my appetite. I felt like a complete joke in front of them, imagining the gossip that was circulating about Diane's *au pair* who freaked over a bottle of *rhum* and one too many guys. Since friendship was out of the question at this point, I swallowed my pride and aimed for professional, and offered the girls something to drink (albeit water). They declined politely, though they were not overly friendly, lest their air of coolness be interrupted. They stood on the other side of the counter from where I chopped, unbothered by my presence. I tried to act nonchalant, uninterested by their *petite fête.*

I concentrated instead on the pleasurable smells of ratatouille, losing myself in the music of my thoughts and the girls' effervescent exchange of French words. Now don't get me wrong—I love America. In fact, I never loved it more than while in the midst of my French experience. But there is no language more beautiful than French. We say, "Good night"; they say, "*Bonsoir.*" We say, "Nice to meet you"; they say, "*Enchantée.*" It's not just the words; it's the sounds—sounds that I tried so hard and failed so miserably to imitate. It's as if there's air blended into the sounds of the vowels and consonants and it lingers between the words. Some French, the French of the butchers, the bakers, the produce men, is guttural, honking right in your face. Then there's the pretty, airy kind that skates in a single, flawless line from one consonant to the next. Diane and her friends spoke the pretty kind, and they sounded so adult doing it. So I listened to them, understanding nothing, wondering exactly how early they all grew up.

It never failed to surprise me how easily they said, "We're taking the *métro*," and hopped from one side of the city to the next like it's normal for girls their age to gallivant through Paris as if it were their own backyard. Then I realized it *was* their backyard, which made them seem even cooler. Then again, considering that their language and their city are birthrights, it wasn't really fair, was it, to elevate them to such a high caste within the realm of female coolness? So I instead considered the *how*, not the *what*. *How* they spoke, *how* they ran around. Correction: they flitted, or sauntered around, more so than ran. It was all wrapped up in an entirely different culture of mannerisms, one that can't be taught or aspired to. Like people who try to be classy—if effort is involved it's simply not so. I was thinking all of this as I turned to grab a soup pot from the cabinet. When I looked back, they were gone.

From the other room, I thought I heard one of them say "we're taking the *métro*." Just as I was about to call out to them, I heard a commotion. I walked out of the kitchen to find three guys climbing through the window. Yes—the window. They were similar in grungy, slimy appearance to the last herd I'd shooed out after the *rhum* incident. Two looked unfamiliar, the other I recognized from Diane's morning-after tryst.

"Hel-looo!" One of them hollered at me, in a pathetic attempt to sound American. I couldn't tell if he was hitting on me or just mocking my existence in general, and either way it didn't matter. I was disgusted.

"He-eyy," the other two said, cooing and smiling in my direction as they climbed through the window into the huge, pristine living room as if it were something they did every day.

Diane et cie., completely unhindered by my presence, pranced down the steps into the living room. It was clear they had been expecting guests. They giggled and preened in front of the boys, who looked them up and down appraisingly. The girls all stood, shuffling their feet, hanging their heads in shy flirtation, laughing, talking, just hanging out with the living room windows wide open and footprints on Alex's sofa, which had been covered with animal skin he'd brought back from an African safari hunt. Why these young beauties found any flattery in the attention of such ill-mannered slugs, I could not imagine.

Rather than inquire about the situation, I shot Diane a stare of death that I hoped she knew meant *Get them out of here. Now.*

She smiled saucily in reply, taking her merry time to casually breeze into the scene, and the calculated coolness I had admired just moments earlier seemed immature, ugly . . . and dangerous. These kids were not elegant or mysterious—they were teenagers. They were cold and utterly disrespectful and I felt my temperature rising. I'd put up with too much from Diane lately, and I wasn't going to take it for another second.

First things first, the babies were not to be witnesses. So I quickly shut the door that led to my nanny basement. Hopefully they were in my room, curled up, unaware, enjoying their afternoon of cinema.

"Diane, I need to talk to you—*now*," I said. I was so angry that my voice was shaking. Shaking and angry or not, it didn't seem to phase the group. They hung their heads and snickered at me, but made no move to leave. Whether they were laughing at my ridiculous Franglais or my red face, I didn't know. And I didn't care.

I didn't care about waiting for Estelle to "have a serious talk" with Diane. I didn't care when she was leaving for Spain. I didn't care about anything. The only thing I did care about was that I wasn't going to tolerate another minute of this. It was all too much, and I couldn't take it anymore. Diane hesitated just a fraction of a second too long before responding, and I lost it.

"Okay. Everybody *out. Now,"* I screamed in a mangled mix of French and English. "Diane, your friends need to leave. Now. This is not okay!" There was stunned silence for a second or two, then the entire group burst into laughter at my Franglais. Words may have failed me, but my body

language did not. I kept my death gaze on Diane, whose expression sobered once she realized I was not backing down.

I clenched my teeth and walked, with what I hoped was considerable composure, into the dining room where the girls had dropped their little pink corduroy blazers, fighting the urge to hurl them down the entryway steps and scream my head off until the little punks ran out the front door. Instead, I walked as calmly as my quivering legs would allow me to the front door, and held the jackets out until the girls collected them in a civilized manner, one by one. I held the door open to show them clearly that they were to take their jackets and keep walking.

I felt abused, underestimated, unappreciated, and invisible. Oh, there would be a lot of head-shaking about this when Maria Celeste came in for her next shift. *Oui! C'est pas bon!!*

At least now the mystery was solved as to how the boyfriend got in for a sleepover. I wanted to call someone to solder shut that window—every window, as a matter of fact. All of a sudden I felt like the dad in *Girls Just Want to Have Fun* who cuts down the tree outside Sarah Jessica Parker's bedroom window so she can't sneak out. Oh, I would be sawing right now if a tree had been the problem.

"Diane, I want you to shut and lock those living room windows *now*," I ordered. "And guys, you can leave through the door and not think about *ever* climbing in here again." They didn't laugh at, nor question my authority. They just left the house without saying another word. After the last one stepped outside, I shut the door and locked it. Then I turned to Diane, feeling very guilty for my outburst. I never knew my boundaries with her, what expectations Estelle had, how Estelle would have wanted me to handle it. I felt wrong to ignore it and wrong to control it. But guilt or not, I still wasn't finished.

"Diane, do you have any idea how much that sofa cost—or the curtains that could have ripped when they climbed *through the windows?*" She looked back at me blankly, and said nothing. I couldn't blame her. I was drained and quite frankly sick of hearing my own voice. "Neither do I," I answered for both of us. "But we both know what your dad would do if he had any idea what has just happened in his living room." She just shrugged. We both sighed. There was no benefit to further discussion.

"Okay—just go to your room, please," I said, softening my voice a bit. And for the first time since I'd been in charge of her, Diane did what she was told.

Somehow the ratatouille didn't sound so good anymore. I left the vegetables strewn across the counter in the kitchen and retreated from the mess I'd made, hobbling, like a soldier wounded in battle, down the basement steps to the nanny room. I found Constantin curled up in my bed, thumb in mouth, glued to the French version of *Lilo et Stitch.* Léonie had discovered how to use my laptop and was frantically typing as she corresponded with her cyber social circle. I knew Estelle wouldn't approve, but non-educational television and Internet over-usage were the least of my worries, so I made room for myself on the bed with Constantin. I asked Léonie to wake me when the movie was over, and as I settled into bed, my eyes filled with tears. I lay there silently and let them fall.

Estelle must have sensed my frustration with the world because the next morning she informed me that the kids and I would be going to her parents' house in Beaune for a *petits vacances*, where in addition to Léonie and Constantin, I would care for Estelle's sister's three children. Estelle worried this would be too much for me, but I was relieved. I needed a vacation from Paris. Too many things had gone wrong and I was starting to feel like I didn't belong. I was ill equipped to raise a teenager and tired of comparing myself to the perfect women of Paris. As sad as it was, nothing had played as I had imagined when I dreamed of Paris from my tiny cube at the *Chronicle*. The city, the language, the children—everything went against my expectations. But it was more than that, it was me. I didn't belong in Paris. I was exhausted. My pre–grad school last hurrah had turned from a dream vacation into a reason I needed another vacation. *Quel nightmare.*

Diane was leaving for Spain early the next morning and according to Estelle, I was supposed to take her shopping for some last-minute necessities. The exchanges between Diane and me thus far had been less than pleasant and I did not expect this outing to go any more smoothly. To avoid deluding myself once again, I put it out of my mind that this trip would be anything close to the girlish play date I'd envisioned when I first came to Paris. But on the other hand, Diane was leaving the country, and I was leaving *for* the country. This was my last chance to forge a friendship between us, and I wanted to do my best to mend the rift, wish her farewell, and wash the whole experience from my mind. Then I would start over with a new focus—the French country.

As Estelle stood in the kitchen, providing directions to the train station and rattling off the last-minute items Diane needed for her trip, a single question ran through my head: *Have any "talks" taken place yet?*

I didn't bring up the episode from the day before, nor did I inquire about *the talk*. I was not a member of the Vladesco family, and I certainly couldn't tell Estelle how to raise her own daughter. Besides, Estelle was obviously distracted—Diane's trip to Spain was a big deal. Estelle hurried about, checking items off of the to-do list. Diane simply hung around the house, counting the hours until her departure. And Alex planned a dinner. He called it a special farewell dinner, and for it, both he and Estelle planned early arrivals home that night. With these events mounting, it was easy for me to hide the complaints I knew I should have expressed.

So this morning I took my morning espresso from Estelle and sipped it while she talked. It was in all our best interests for me to stay quiet. No one here wanted the special farewell dinner spoiled. Still, I worried about what would happen next. The *rhum*, the overnight guests, the sneaking around—if all of these things were happening when Diane was fourteen, what would happen when she was fifteen? Or sixteen? And if her mother never talked to her about her behavior, how much worse would it get? And what would become of her after I passed out of her life? I tried to push these thoughts out of my head as I nodded and smiled my way through Estelle's light-hearted morning chatter. Once I wished her a lovely day, I sat in the kitchen, getting skinny and high off espresso, waiting for Diane to wake up.

Léonie and Constantin were spending the day with Mounie *et* Mip to play golf. I pictured Léonie perfecting her swing, sort of the way I pictured Jordan Baker in the *Great Gatsby*. Léonie could definitely grow up to be a Jordan— slightly feminist, cool but elegant, sporty but beautiful. But instead of clear, gray eyes, Léonie's eyes were dark and deep; instead of blond hair, Léonie's was dark and curly; and instead of a tanned, healthy glow, Léonie possessed flawless, porcelain skin. She was studied and serious, and I knew she would push her limits on the golf course to a raised standard of perfection, whether or not it was her first time.

Then I pictured Constantin standing next to her, with golf club in hand. I was very grateful I would not have to take responsibility for the destruction of whatever he swung at.

Then my thoughts turned back to Diane. Ever since she had traded my girl-bonding daydreams for boys and a rum buzz, I wanted her approval and mutual acceptance even more than I normally would. The shopping trip was a good start, but I was nervous about it. I wondered whether she was dreading it, what she thought of me, and mostly what on earth we would talk about. After all, we exchanged most of our conversation in the form of sighs and dirty looks. Still, I was determined to make things right between us.

Diane finally rolled downstairs at almost noon, ready to go though not overly zealous about it. I did my best to contain my own excitement, like the nerdy girl in school who had to pretend it was no big deal to get invited to the cool girls' Friday night sleepover. I gave her what I hoped was a friendly smile and checked the house purse, which held only 50 euros. Definitely not enough. I went to my room and dug into my own stash, knowing Estelle would refund me later.

I'm embarrassed to admit it, but the entire time I was in Paris, I had no idea what I was getting paid. I've never been much of a numbers person, and with the confusion of living in a *new* house and getting paid in foreign money, plus the fact that all of my daily nannying duties were funded by the house purse, I couldn't even begin to guess how much I'd made up until that point. All I knew was that each week, the stack of bills in the envelope got thicker and thicker, and I hadn't even had the chance to spend it yet. I may not have been a numbers person, but I was a shopping person. I had no doubt I'd find a use for the cash long before I returned to my home sweet home across the pond.

I grabbed 100 more euros, just in case Diane's necessities turned into Diane's frivolous wants. I was not afraid to admit that I would try to buy her affection, if that's what it took. It wasn't until we were halfway to the *métro* that I realized I'd left my debit card at home and hadn't grabbed any extra cash for myself. As we walked along, Diane was cool and I was cautious, nervous and unsure of the train route Diane insisted we take. I felt like a complete mom, a no-fun mom at that, and that was an image I had never wanted to exude.

Diane's train route led us to a different train station than the *métro* I was accustomed to taking. I had no choice but to follow nervously behind her, trusting she had ridden this train before, probably one too many times. She walked to the ticket counter several strides in front of me, as if *I* were the child and *she* were the adult. And as I suspected, she knew exactly where to go, exactly what to do, exactly what tickets to buy, and exactly how much those tickets cost. It was only when she turned to me for money to pay for the tickets that I remembered who was in charge, and I handed her the cash, slightly dampened by my palm. We found seats on the RER train. I sat in a seat by the window and she sat in the seat that faced me, but she stared out the window almost immediately after sitting down.

Despite her recent acts of defiance, Diane looked quite sweet sitting across from me on the train—almost like a little girl. I wondered if she knew how pretty she was. She probably did. But good, she should know. I tried to think of something to say to her. If I was trying to strike up conversation with any other fourteen-year-old girl, most likely I would have asked, *"Soooo . . . do you have a boyfriend?"* This question, however, was entirely off-limits. I knew more about the answer than I cared to, and I wasn't emotionally strong enough to hear any more details about it. Not that she would have told me, anyway. Even though I had only been in her life for two weeks and most of our relationship had been rocky, I was determined to relate to her in some way. I was in her life and she was in mine in this given moment and I wanted that to matter—to both of us. I just had to figure out a way to make it happen.

We rode in silence and I wondered how many nannies

had been in and out of her life, forcing her to say hello and good-bye to a new face every year. How many summers had she spent under the care of a stranger? How many mornings had she walked herself to school because the nanny had to walk her younger sister and brother to a different school? As I watched her look sullenly at her own reflection, suddenly I didn't feel so intimidated anymore. For all of her adult talk and adult actions, she *was* still a little girl; she'd just been forced to grow up very fast. She coped with it the only way she knew how, and quite frankly coped better than I surely would have in the same situation. And then I smiled.

She noticed, and turned away from the window to face me. She shrugged and her delicate shoulders sunk inward. I smiled straight at her, looking her in the eyes with as much affection as I could deliver. It was my attempt at holding out an olive branch. She stared back, and for a moment, I thought she wouldn't reciprocate. Then her face broke into a smile, and she let out a short puff of breath, somewhere between a sigh of relief and a laugh. I realized that maybe all this time she had wanted my approval as much as I'd wanted hers. The ice was broken. My shoulders relaxed and the tightness I'd felt in my chest disappeared.

"Are you nervous about going to Spain?" I asked.

"Uhhh, no," she said. I laughed. Of course she wasn't.

"Have you been before?" I asked.

"Uhhh, yeah," she said.

I nodded, not knowing how to drive the conversation further, but determined to get past the uncomfortable pauses.

"But have you been to—what city are you going to?" I asked.

"It's by the sea, that's all I know," she said. "So I need a new swimsuit."

Estelle had listed the swimsuit as one of the necessities we needed to buy Diane. I couldn't imagine she didn't already have several, with all the weekly scuba lessons and coastal family vacations. But okay, we'd buy a swimsuit.

We talked on, plodding through the awkward barrier that had divided us for the past several weeks. Diane told me about all of the countries she'd been to, and as she talked of family vacations and summer camps, her expression warmed. She grinned as she talked and kept her hands free to gesture, saying "so" and "yeah" and "okay" at the start of each sentence. I was struck by how much she was like each of her parents. I had never realized how much she was like her father, expressive, eager, even using the word *"bon"* as Alex did to commence her every thought. But when she talked I heard Estelle in her voice. It had that deep, muffled tone possessed by those *parisiens* who spoke the beautiful kind of French. All French women—particularly the ones who are mysterious, beautiful, and effortlessly cool—spoke the beautiful French with a beautiful voice. Diane talked on, the corners of her mouth curled upward in the same coy smile of her mother— of a French woman.

As the *métro* pulled into rue de Passy, Diane assured me it was the absolute best place to shop in Paris, and chattered excitedly about all of the stores, from Gap to Guerlain.

We paid tribute to Kookai, H&M, and a few couture bou-tiques. Diane purchased a tiny yellow string bikini trimmed in sequins that had about as much material as something I would wear around my wrist. *Très necessaire, non?* She also se-lected a couple of paper-thin camisoles that should not have been worn as shirts. I was sure though, that she would, and dared not think about what activities could follow.

In between shops, we stopped at a *petite patisserie*, where I bought a pastry resembling an American lemon square. We shared it as we walked on to Zara. I am convinced that Zara was made for me. I love to shop, but I've always been easily overwhelmed by the sheer number of choices. But since Zara organizes all inventory—from clothes to shoes—by color, I just pick a color (usually black) and go for it. Walking into the store, I was hit by a wave of homesickness, and it was only enhanced by the mostly American soundtrack playing on the sound system. When "Hungry Eyes" came on, I squealed "*Dirty Dancing!*" to Diane, but she responded only with a blank look. She'd never heard of nor seen the movie. A tragedy! I made a mental note to myself that should we have time after she returned from Spain, we would watch that movie together at least once.

There's nothing like good music to make me shop like a madwoman, and even my lack of cash flow couldn't stop me from grabbing up every black stiletto, black dress, and black flare-leg pant Zara had to offer. I hummed along to the music, imagining Patrick Swayze and Baby rehearsing for that famous mambo number. The Ally McBeal inside me was tempted to start a mambo number of my own on top of the center table display when I realized that once again, my coolness level needed a check.

By the time we'd finished our shopping, we were late for dinner. I felt satisfied as Diane and I raced home together. We had accomplished our primary mission but I couldn't help but feel that a much bigger mission had also been accomplished. We were friends. I was even glad we were running late just so she knew I wasn't really the type of person who always had to follow the rules. I hated that I'd come off that way to her, and to myself.

When we returned home, Alex was conducting a grand orchestra of gourmet in the kitchen, and the mood in the house was a happy one. We ate a five-course meal, ending with a farewell toast to Diane. She drank a full glass of champagne, laughing and cooing with her mother all the while. Before I retreated to my basement room for the night, I left a little good-bye note on Diane's pillow. It was the final gesture in my efforts to cancel out whatever negativity carried over from our rocky start. I stood in her room for just a few moments, looking at the girlish notes and pictures decorating every square inch of the wall. My heart went out to her. I breathed in deeply, hoping to freeze time and perhaps preserve whatever of her young years remained. Minutes later, once down in my nanny room, she instant-messaged me from her bedroom on the third floor under the screen name DiDi14. She couldn't wait to watch *Dirty Dancing* when she got home from Spain, her message said. I beamed. I would have it waiting here for her. I wrote her back to tell her and went to sleep relieved and heart-warmed that we had found friendship.

My time in Paris was nearly complete. I had served my purpose and was closer to being a nanny in good standing. The French country waited, and that thought alone assured me I belonged in no other place.

Chapitre Huit

French country. In America, it's the inspiration for Lenox china patterns—clean, white, classic. It's a motif of home décor—toile in the dining room, roosters in the kitchen. It's linen. It's quilted. Fabrics of yellows, reds, and oranges draped over solid oak tables or spread over a featherbed of down, tucked into white-washed iron bedposts. It's a pleasant retreat, visiting a home decked in French country is; made perfect by the lingering fragrance of lavender-scented linen spray. I should know—I own a bottle for my sheets and towels.

Back in America, when I'd browsed through Williams-Sonoma, looking lustfully at the full line of Emile Henry ovenware, it never really occurred to me that French country design was inspired by an actual place, namely Provence. Safe under the shelter of retail America, I divided my love of French country equally between the au gratin pans and the soup terrines, careful to avoid the blinding glare of the overhead fluorescent lights that bounced off the dishes' glossy ceramic glaze. I visited there often and browsed till my heart was content luxuriating in the store's air-conditioning, which always remained at a cool and constant sixty-five degrees.

But in France, French country isn't just the design for a line of cookware. It is a place *en plein-air* where one hunts—*sans* air-conditioning—for wild boar, mushrooms, and modern plumbing. And when considering the latter, it's a fact that the smell lingering amidst the great outdoors is anything but lavender.

When Estelle first mentioned I would take the kids to their grandparents' house in Burgundy, I found myself instantly enamored with the glamorous thought of ten days in the French country. What I didn't realize at the time, of course, is that whether Burgundian or Provençal, there is no bottled spray that could prepare me for the realities of being a city girl thrown to the foxes and hounds of country living. So I approached the journey the best way I knew how: I planned my outfit for the first day.

I scoured my closet of clothes, most of which had hung unworn since I'd arrived in Paris. After my first day on the job, I'd all but chucked the effort to be fashionable in favor of concentrating on completing my nanny duties without burning the house down. But the country, I reasoned, would be more relaxed, thus allowing me to leisurely groom myself and dress in style. For the train ride to Burgundy, I chose a crisp white button-down shirt and camel-colored wool gabardine pants. I topped it off with my berry-colored cashmere cable V-neck from Brooks Brothers to adopt a true country appeal, casual and comfortable at the same time. I hated to be so provincial in suede loafer flats, but I had a feeling that kitten heels wouldn't tread well on vineyard soil, and I was anticipating long walks through the age-old famous vineyards of Beaune. I pulled the ensemble together with a silk Coach scarf with pink trim.

The morning of our departure, I decided to celebrate with a last tribute to Paris—lunch at Paul. Paul was my favorite bread shop in the city, and I loved it despite the fact that it was a chain restaurant, revealing my hopelessly American sensibilities. But I couldn't resist the charming décor, I considered it an appropriate segue from city to country life— from breads, to hardwoods, to copper antiques, to walls painted every shade of caramel, wheat, and pecan. Thick, rustic oak shelves lined the back wall, where woven baskets of straw housed loaf upon loaf of bread. Some were speckled with grains, some porous in texture, some were flat, some, called *boules*, were shaped as round as basketballs. The bread decorated the shelves, overflowed from the baskets, and lay stacked on the countertops to prove true the slogan of Paul, the passion of bread for 116 years: *"La passion du pain depuis 116 ans."* The baguettes, though, were separate from the rest. They stood alone, half as tall as me, in barreled baskets on the ground. I was tempted to tear off hunks to chew as I waited in line with the kids who were equally drooling. But since my first visit to Paul, I owed my loyalty to *Le Dieppois*, a signature choice from the *collection de sandwiches Paul*. It was a simple combination of tuna, lettuce, and tomato, but of course the bread kept me coming back for more.

Constantin, while disappointed that a large variety of

saucisson did not accompany the selection of sandwiches, quiches, pizzas, and tarts behind the glass counter, settled for the next best thing, *Le Savoreux,* a sandwich of *rosette,* or salami, *et beurre.* Léonie, as classic as they come, ordered her favorite of *jambon et beurre,* ham on buttered bread. The name of it suited her as much as it suited the components of the sandwich, *Le Parisien.* We found seats in the back of the store along the bar. The two kids, who hardly pushed around an ounce of pasta and a few peas during a normal weekday dinner, devoured their sandwiches, which were easily the length from my elbow to fingertips. Constantin sat humming and gabbing about what he "can" do once we arrived in Beaune, while Léonie corrected his grammar and whispered to me how excited she was to see her cousin Jeanne. Jeanne was the oldest of Estelle's sister's kids and would be in Beaune by the time we arrived, along with her two little brothers, Joseph and Auguste. I looked forward to meeting them all, and hoped I would be as delighted by them as I was by Léonie and Constantin, who munched their bread and butter as they talked and giggled together about their summer adventures.

La Gare de Lyon, the gateway to the East, was magnificent in structure, and I gawked at the high ceilings and muted light as we made our way through the station with our luggage. The kids were unaffected by the grandness of the station. Train travel was so common in Europe that it was likely the kids had taken, in their short lives, more trains than I had planes. But for me, whose knowledge of train travel came solely from movies about Montana and novels about the

American dream, the idea of traveling to Burgundy by train prompted thoughts of romance and European intrigue.

Léonie insisted on charging ahead as usual, as we scoured the platforms for the train going from Paris to Dijon, Dijon to Beaune. I clutched Constantin close to my side and kept an eye on Léonie as we were swiped, bumped, and nudged by the dozens of travelers bustling in every direction. Whistles blew, engines chugged, announcements *en français* rang overhead, though the echoing commotion of frenzied travelers and hundreds of conversations happening all at once rendered the overhead announcements all but impossible to understand.

Waving her hand in the direction of our platform, Léonie ran back to beg me to let her punch our tickets. "I always do it," she insisted. Unaware our tickets even needed punching, I was glad to pretend to delegate the task and ignore the fact that an eleven-year-old was more competent than me. The conductor stood on the platform outside the train, greeting each passenger with a jovial grin and firm nod. As we approached, Constantin, expecting above-average treatment, extended his small hand with utmost confidence. *"Bonjour!"* he said, standing strong before the conductor who, winking at me, offered a hearty handshake and a *"Bonjour"* in return. I smiled back at the conductor, a secret exchange from one adult to another, both of us humored by the child's unknowingly provided entertainment.

Léonie was first to board and again took charge, promptly loading the red canvas suitcase she and Constantin shared onto the luggage rack. I fumbled along behind, pulling Constantin and my trunk, which was big enough to contain one year's worth of travel attire. Constantin squirmed from my grip, stubborn and reluctant to follow, as he clearly wanted to retain his place beside the conductor to continue a cordial exchange as passengers boarded. I forced him otherwise onto the train, smiling again at the indulgent conductor. Léonie and Constantin were already engrossed in a game of magnetic travel checkers when I came back from double-checking that our luggage was stored safely. I sat back in my coach seat feeling appropriately dressed and amply prepared to depart from the city behind us. There was nothing left for me to do but relax, at last. I stared out the window to my left, shuffling through the thoughts I'd forced to the recesses of my mind since becoming the *au pair des Vladesco*. It seemed like it was ages ago that anything occupied my mind besides grocery shopping, thin French women, and teenage drama.

I sighed in exhaustion as the train pulled out of the station. The whistle blew and I exhaled with it, watching the graffiti of the Paris train station walls disappear as the outskirts of the city, *les banlieues*, spread for miles outside the window. We accelerated and the concrete and steel of the buildings outside gave way to industrial parks, which gave way to sloping valleys and pleasant pastures, until we reached the 254 kilometer per hour speed of the *train à grande vitesse*, the TGV. I leaned my head back against the seat, inhaled and exhaled long and slow breaths, and let thoughts of summertime vacation wash over me. I stared at the passing scenery until all that was visible through the windows were stripes of blurry greens.

We zoomed forward to Dijon. Léonie and Constantin were now engrossed in an electronic form of Hangman. I sat still and quiet, wondering how the grandparents would receive me. Léonie said I was the first of their nannies to stay the night with them in Beaune. I wondered how their cousins would receive me; they were from Bergerac in Dordogne, a region in Southwest France, and I doubted they spoke English as well as Léonie and Constantin, if at all. I wondered what the home of French wine millionaires looked like—and what I would look like in it. Mostly, I wondered whether I would be a better fit in the country than I had been in Paris. I wanted to love Paris—and I did—but I had failed so miserably there, day after day. Perhaps the country—still, small and *un petit plus* old-fashioned—would suit me better.

Constantin whined. I heard him fussing over what he "could do" in this game of Hangman; the rules according to Constantin. I gave him a quick *shhsh*, like Donna Reed might do whenever her otherwise perfect children exhibited typical childish behavior. In the two weeks I'd known them, I'd completely fallen in love with them, and when we were all out together, I often wondered if the people around us thought they were my children. I wanted to look old enough to be their mother but still appear young and beautiful all the same. I wanted to know them well enough to have them mind me, respect me, and despite discipline and impatience, love me at the end of the day.

My feelings toward the children made my heart ache in a way it never had before, and I wondered when I would have my own children who would love me unconditionally, who looked to me for support and guidance. And once I did, would I finally be satisfied?

All my life I'd fluttered along, not really knowing where I belonged. My mom used to call me her "elusive butterfly." It drove me crazy but at the same time I sort of loved it. It made me feel free and untouchable. I felt able to fly to any place at any time. And so I did. I searched for self-worth in anything that would distract me from looking where I should really find it—from Kate Spade shoes to unfulfilling jobs, and even coming to Paris. And even though I'd traveled across an ocean and was living a world away from the life I'd always known, I still didn't know what I wanted. But I knew I wanted to work toward something with meaning, something that would fulfill me, give me purpose, keep me going. Until I could give birth to my own children (under the covenant of holy matrimony, of course), getting my master's degree seemed like the perfect *something*. It sounded so good—it sounded rational and even grown-up. But was it yet another misguided search to find satisfaction in something that wasn't right for me? Not that living (let alone marrying) for the sake of childbirth was any better, but dadgum my biological clock. I swore I felt like fertile Mother Earth since I was thirteen years old.

Looking at Léonie and Constantin across the aisle from me, so beautiful, so sweet, so well behaved, I gave in and pretended for a few more minutes that they were mine. I knew in my gut that having children would not fill my emptiness, make me feel beautiful, or give me a sense of identity or purpose—any more than an engagement ring on my left hand would. But what would? I was starting to believe grad school was just another temporary fix, my own sought-after self-importance. But if an acceptance letter didn't come, I had no idea what to do next.

The train slowed, turning the blurry greens and browns to recognizable hillsides once again. The hillsides became whole villages. Storybook villages, with a bell tower, a church steeple, a chimney poking from the center of the rooftops. Then the villages gave way to modern suburban communities. And in no time, graffiti appeared on the cement wall just outside my window. Dijon.

I let the kids wander around the cabin while passengers exited and new ones boarded. These travelers were the type who only seemed to appear on these journeys. Their clothing was more rumpled than their Parisian counterparts, their hair more disheveled, and they had a distinctly stale odor. In other words, they were undoubtedly European. I watched them and wondered what their stories were. I wondered how many of them saw me with two beautiful children and envied my place in life, as I certainly envied the image I was presenting.

We settled in for the final, shorter leg of the trip. The train was quieter, the crowd lighter than before. I gave Constantin and Léonie candy I'd been hiding in my purse, a substitute for the *goûter* they missed today, and an effort to postpone the whining about near-dinnertime hunger pangs. We arrived *à la Gare de Beaune* at 5 p.m. Mamie, as the children call their grandmother, and Léonie's favorite cousin, Jeanne, greeted us there. While Mamie was the childrens' affectionate name for their grandmother, when pronounced *en français,* it sounded too close to "Mommy" in English, so I greeted her formally as Madame Marion.

Jeanne was beautiful with darker skin and hair, and more of a seriousness about the eyes than my darling Léonie. She also looked much older than Léonie, bigger in frame and stature, though they were about the same age. Jeanne was shy, and stood back from the scene a bit, not unlike Léonie on the first day we met. Knowing it would take time to draw her out, I hastened to greet her warmly and with open arms, hoping to overcome any initial barriers. Madame Marion was much more outgoing than her granddaughter. She was fresh, lively, and pleased to welcome three more to her already full house. She stood erect, wearing a black linen sundress, her tanned skin stretched taut over toned arms and a thin face. Briskly she shook my hand, which was sweating along with the rest of me as a result of my ill-timed sweater/blouse combo. We walked on through the gravelly train station parking lot to the car, one of those tiny European ones that would never survive on the road next to the SUVs of America. Madame Marion wore white, closed-toe mules and is the only woman I've seen to date who has pulled it off charmingly.

I should have known a Frenchwoman always wears heels, thus providing me with my first inkling that perhaps we wouldn't spend our afternoons and evenings walking the vineyards after all.

We all piled into the tiny car, and I wondered how it was not against safety codes to cram so many bodies in such a small space. It was warmer than I thought it would be and I was forced to remove my Coach scarf from my neck. As I did so, I was reminded of my first day in Paris—how all of the primping in the airport bathroom had proved fruitless in the face of city heat. There I was not five minutes into my country experience and I'd already lost my equestrian-wannabe, country-by-catalogue, effortlessly classy appeal. Without my signature scarf, I was merely a stuffy, seasonally overdressed girl in a pink sweater and camel-colored pants. And next to Madame Marion, the wife of a wine millionaire who just breezed along with her grandchildren looking as though she'd just stepped from the pages of a magazine, I clashed completely with her style and charisma.

We drove around the *centre ville*, and Madame Marion pointed out the stunning *château* of Chanson, which had belonged to the Marion family for centuries before they sold it. Then we pulled through an electronic gate into the current *chez Marion*, a surprisingly modern structure painted in bright oranges and pale yellows, with wide white stone steps leading to the front door. Monsieur Marion, Joseph, and Auguste greeted us from the front steps. Until that moment, it hadn't really registered that during my time in the country, I would be a nanny of five. Jeanne and Léonie were the same age, so I felt no immediate concern to tend to them—they would happily occupy themselves. Joseph was one year younger than them, at age ten. I wasn't exactly sure where he would fit in among the group. He was sweet, with dark hair, skin, and eyes like his older sister. Auguste, the youngest of all at five years of age, stood apart from the others, dazed from the flurry of activity. I greeted him first, and when he smiled, I noticed that his two front teeth were missing. *Charmant!* He had the same tan skin and brown eyes as his brother and sister, but his hair was dirty blond, perhaps yet to turn dark.

Monsieur Marion was the quintessential Frenchman, dressed in dark khaki trousers, a light-colored button-down shirt topped with a houndstooth blazer, and a dark paisley silk scarf wrapped around his neck in a neat cuff. He looked so elegant that I wished I hadn't succumbed to the heat and removed my own scarf, which I'd longed to wear throughout my arrival in the same cuff-like fashion. As we shook hands, I felt an instant affection toward him, very much like the way I would feel toward a grandfather. He had kind eyes, slightly droopy at the corners, capped with bushy eyebrows. A pair of silver-rimmed glasses perched on the bridge of his bulbous, red-veined nose—a nose proficient at wine sniffing, no doubt. I had a feeling we'd get along well. Unlike his more youthful wife, who moved with an ease and grace that defied her age, Monsieur Marion hobbled up the steps to open the door for us all. A gracious host, he assured me that I had my own room and that dinner was just about ready. Something about the steady nod of his head and attentive raising of his bushy eyebrows as he ushered me inside both captivated and relaxed me. I had a feeling I would enjoy the country even more than I'd thought.

Inside, I was pleased to find *les Marion* went against the grain of the rest of France (or Paris, at least), and utilized the modern luxury of air-conditioning. The house was cool and clean, and for the most part free of clutter, a way of life I found more typical of the French the longer I was in their country. The kids immediately dispersed, taking full rein of the house, which seemed an accepted routine. Madame Marion showed me downstairs to my room. We entered the house on the main floor—the *rez-de-chausée*, to be proper—but there was a downstairs where the boys and I would sleep. Mamie *et* Grandpère, along with the girls, would sleep in the rooms upstairs. On the top floor were two other bedrooms that went largely unused. And next to the main house was a kids' clubhouse, built as sturdy as its larger counterpart, but complete with stone walls and shutters.

We had an hour before dinner, so, as Madame Marion had instructed, I unloaded my clothes into the bureau and hung my coats in the armoire in the hall. I decided it wouldn't be too awful if I just lay down for a *petite* rest before dinner-time. I hadn't slept much the night before, as I'd spent half of it planning my outfit, and in the after-midnight hours making international phone calls when, at home in central time, friends and family were just getting off work. I was exhausted. Between the train ride and traveling alone with two kids and all of that luggage, I could have sacked out for the rest of the night. But even thirty minutes would have been a welcome retreat.

I rolled back the white *matelassé* coverlet and climbed beneath the lilac-printed sheets, charmed to discover they really did smell like lavender. The down pillows were large and square, and heavenly relief for my travel-weary head. But I hadn't closed my eyes for more than two minutes when my back bedroom door, which led to the outside courtyard, swung open. I jolted awake in time to see the girls run through the door, through my room, and out the main door into the hallway. They did not slow down or even notice me lying in the bed, and before I could even question their activity, they were gone. Just as I got up to shut both doors, the boys barreled through, hollering in their kiddie French about a chase, and proclaiming victory of boys over girls. Normally, I would have been amused by their antics. But instead, I was just irritated. Great—we'd been in the country less than an hour, and my fantasies of a quiet retreat were already crushed. I longed for a quiet place to lie down, but there wasn't another appropriate place for me to get my beauty sleep, so I gave up and headed to the kitchen to help with dinner preparations.

Mamie was in the kitchen with a half-apron fitted securely over her black linen dress. She was brushing her hands together in quick motion as I peeped my head around the corner. No one spoke English at *chez Marion* except Léonie and Constantin. As humiliating as it would be, I would converse *en français* or not at all.

"*Puis-je vous aider?*" I asked, offering to help the best way I knew how.

"*Bah non,*" the madame replied with a shrug of her shoulders and a graceful flick of her wrist. By her body language and the *au contraire* implication of "*bah,*" I wasn't sure if she really meant I could help or that there was absolutely nothing she needed me to do. Uncertain of my place but wanting to offer my help, I peeked into the dining room to determine whether places had been set. They had. Blast. I hoped the kids had been commissioned for this chore, because if it was my duty and the madame had already taken up my slack, I was down by major points. But the bread was not out. I could cut bread. So back into the kitchen I wandered.

"Uhh, Madame Marion, peut-etre je couper du pain?" I asked in language that disgraced my high school French teacher.

"Bah oui!" the madame replied with almost the same body movement as she had used just minutes ago, when her answer was the opposite.

As I sliced small rounds the madame hurriedly shouted, *"À table,"* to the kids racing in the yard outside. We ate a salmon soufflé and while it did not sound appetizing at first, it was delicious. The more I ate, the more it felt like it had been days since I gobbled *dieppois* from Paul. There was an intense comfort of some sort felt in all of the meals prepared for me in France, as if I were being fed rather than merely eating. By my last bite of soufflé, I felt happy and at ease. By the time we finished dinner, Monsieur Marion, next to whom I sat, had kindly offered me two books, one magazine, and one dictionary to aid my language deficiencies. He assured me that if I chose just one article and mastered it, I would learn the language more quickly than if I tried to browse entire volumes at once. I smiled graciously, knowing that I would be lucky to master one sentence, and that was no understatement. He offered small insights into winemaking, telling me that on the hot days there, on the overcast days there, on the normal days there, he made it his passionate duty to record every aspect of the weather. He recounted which years had the most sun and which the most rain, right down to the day. I listened with humble respect while he pointedly expressed that in the twenty years between 1980 and 2000 there were more hot summers than there were in the eighty years between 1900 and 1980. Then he added a wine aficionado's guide to Burgundy to my reading list and politely dismissed himself from the table, taking one last sip from his glass of red.

I was looking forward to following up the relaxing dinner with a relaxing evening of reading lessons when Madame Marion announced she and the monsieur were leaving for the night. They had a concert to attend outside of town, which meant I was on babysitting duty. I thought of my own grandparents, and how unusual it would have been for them to attend a concert so late in the evening, but it was obvious *les Marion* were the lively kind. And so I was left in charge of five children, three of them total strangers, in an unfamiliar house, with zero instruction on routine bedtime procedures. I should have asked for instructions but of course—in between learning a new dialect of the French language, counting the number of kids, remembering their names, and figuring out exactly what I was doing there—it didn't occur to me to ask for instructions. It was going to be a bumpy night.

After they left, I raided the pantry for chocolate— every French woman keeps a stash of the most bitter, silky kind—and took a seat alone in the kitchen, trying to decide if I should just let the children play outside until dark or force them into bed earlier than ever so that I could get some peace and quiet. As I nibbled my chocolate, I added to my list of French lessons three key phrases of which I'm sure Monsieur

Marion would have approved and Madame Marion would have employed: *on se lave les mains* (wash your hands); *on se douche* (take your baths), and *on se couche* (time for bed).

"On se douche!" I finally yelled out the kitchen windows to the summer-filled children gallivanting through their grandmother's flowerbeds. The girls obeyed without question. The boys, stubborn and not wanting to submit to a bath, fought over who had to go first. Auguste, being the youngest, lost by a landslide. I walked outside to meet him, feeling sorry for the youngest little darling. Abandoned by his siblings and cousins, he stood looking up at me with his toothless grin. I was just wondering if he, like Constantin, would fight me about the bath when, without prompting, he placed his little hand in mine and we walked together to *"on se douche."*

In the bathroom downstairs, which I would be sharing with the three dirty boys, Auguste stood staring at me, still and mute as he had been since I met him. I had no idea what to do next, so I left, in case I was breeching the contract of nanny duties versus mother duties. Seconds later, I called to him from the other side of the bathroom door, "Auguste?"

"Quoi?" he said, drawing out the word in the sweetest, most helpless tone.

"On se douche?" This time it was a question and not a demand. I really needed to find out whether or not he could take his bath alone.

"Non," he replied obediently. So I stepped inside to find the little boy standing completely undressed next to the claw-foot tub with his thumb in his mouth and a confused expression on his face.

"*Je regrette, Auguste. Désolée. Alors, on se douche.*" I said, trying to reassure him I was the clueless one of the two. I started the water, which ran from a hand-held hose attachment. This would not make for pleasant bath times of my own, but I would deal with that later. Auguste climbed in the tub without any instruction, though I saw he was holding one of his tiny, knobby knees with both hands and looked a bit pained. It was bleeding—Constantin no doubt had won a game in the garden earlier. He looked so sweet and confused that all of my anxiety faded and I kissed his sweaty head, which smelled of grass and fresh dirt, and reassured him with my eyes that he would be all better—all clean and better— soon. I found in a bureau by the sink a supply of *savon de la bonne mère,* a soap l'Occitane makes that means "grandma's soap." Mamie had a stash of the *au naturel* scent, which smelled like a combination of butter and honey and milk. I kept the lavender scent in my own bathroom in Houston, but the soap made much more sense here, with grubby little boys swiping it back and forth on their tiny hands after a long day of play, yelling "Mamie!" The l'Occitane slogan is "A True Story," and after my time in the country, I finally understood the image they intended.

Once we'd washed and scrubbed and bandaged wounds and gotten the little tyke all dry and dressed in his button-down pjs, I turned my attention to the others. One by one, I got them to bathe, and then, after chasing boys and girls through the house and checking for brushed teeth and clean hair, I felt at last able and accomplished enough to move them on to the next stage of the nighttime ritual.

Rachel Spencer

"On se couche," I called.

Auguste had not left my side since bath time, and he was so small and quiet that I worried he wouldn't want to sleep alone. But when we walked hand in hand to his bedroom, he stopped next to his bedside and looked at me quizzically. "Okay, Auguste, *on se couche,"* I repeated gently, patting his back in the direction of the bed and expecting a Constantin-like bedtime struggle. But before I could reach over him to turn out the light, he crawled into his bed, cupped his hands and the edge of his blanket under his chin, and shut his little eyes to sleep. I could see the gap where his two front teeth should be through his slightly parted lips. He'd instantly obeyed me—I was baffled. And my heart melted. He could not have been more adorable.

Chapitre Neuf

The next morning was market day in the *centre ville de Beaune*, and I had been invited to accompany Madame Marion on her weekly trip. We left the house early while the sky was still gray, and I wondered if it would rain. I followed the madame the few shorts blocks to the *centre ville*. She kept up a brisk stride, even while pulling the sizeable basket behind her. In both the city and the country, the French women transport their produce purchases in stroller-like grocery carts. Some are canvas bags with a wire frame, some are of sturdy woven straw bound at the top with leather straps. All of them are on wheels, making it easy to roll them home from the market.

The market was spread in every direction of the town's main square. Madame invited me to watch as she picked out her selections, but also encouraged me to explore on my own. Afraid of getting lost, I stayed beside her and observed, humored, as she, like the rest, handled every fruit, vegetable, jar, or bushel before selecting the best crop. At the cheese stand, the farmer was dressed in a white-and-black-striped long-sleeve shirt, with a red handkerchief tied around his neck. He

Rachel Spencer

wore a black engineer's cap on his head of unkempt gray-streaked hair that matched his beard of the same color. He had the same eyes as Monsieur Marion, drooping at the sides, pushed down by heavy, dark, bushy eyebrows. At his stand was a long row of wooden crates all full of darling rounds of *chèvre,* some wrapped in wax paper, some out for tasting. Some were herbed and some *au cendre,* encased in ash, as Alex prefers. There was a wooden board standing up behind the crates that read C'EST LE PRODUIT DE NOTRE FERME, or "this is the product of our farm." The words were painted in black inside a drawn talking bubble that extended from the mouth of a cartoon goat. Monsieur Chèvre chuckled when he saw me staring perplexed at his cartoon goat.

"*C'est vrai, non?*" he asked, jesting that the talking goat was as real a part of his display as he himself.

"*Voilà—un goûter!*" he said, handing me a pinch from one of the herbed *crottins.* I smiled in gratitude and let the creamy tartness, followed by a hint of rosemary, wash over my tongue. The flavors melded together, and the intense fresh-ness of it seemed unlikely from a cheese so dry and crumbly. The madame had wandered to another booth to inspect fresh bundles of green-leaf lettuce, and I moved to follow her.

"*Merci, monsieur,*" I said, waving good-bye to my new friend and wishing for *un rétro* upon which to slather at least five *crottins* at once. I arrived at Madame's side just in time to see her reject the lettuce farmer's rather wilted-looking offer-ings and move on to the next stall where, *on peut espérer,* she settled upon lettuce with much less dirt caked at the base and far perkier green leaves. Madame made her marketplace purchases efficiently and encouraged me to roam the crowds of Saturday morning in downtown Beaune. I breathed in the morning air, thick with rain about to fall, absorbing as much as one could of the history and wonderment of the ancient structures around me. The buildings were stacked right up against each other as if they were joined by brick and mortar, though their rooftops stood at many different heights, and their stone walls were varied shades of faded grays and browns. The buildings of Beaune had a much humbler appeal than their more lavishly carved Parisian counterparts. The people were humbler, too. There was a gentleness in the air, a warmth and companionship not present on the bustling streets of Paris. I felt at ease walking among crowds of gray-haired folks—grandmothers and grandfathers, most likely—mingling together in their gray-haired town. I could almost feel the centuries of stories. Small stories, but great ones.

I came upon a poster display of vintage champagne advertisements cluttered on the surfaces of several tables in the bit of the market designated for antiques, heirlooms, and other rare finds. I browsed the posters and found two black-and-white ads, one from the forties, one from the fifties, both of a nearby vineyard on down the Côte d'Or from Beaune. I purchased them for 12 euros exactly. It was practically the first purchase I'd made for myself, other than food, since coming to France.

I left the Saturday market to the jubilant ringing of bagpipes and Scottish dancers in the square. They danced to the music with jubilant clicking of heels, winking at the passers-by as if at one time or another they'd shared a secret or a mug of ale. I caught the glimmer in one's eye as she winked and nodded to a serious-looking gentleman walking under the shelter of a black umbrella. I hoped for her own good cheer he smiled back.

Walking home in the misty rain, clutching my new prized possessions, I wondered what day it would be that I would visit the vineyard captured in these posters, taste the wine, walk the soil. For now, it was nearly lunchtime and I would again feast at *chez Marion* with fine company and the finest Beaune wine I'd tasted yet. At dinner the night before, Monsieur Marion revealed three labels I had not seen at Alex and Estelle's, and I had since looked forward to even more discoveries. The variety was greater in Beaune, and the bottles more aged. I inhaled the wet residue of the morning, whetting my palette for a new bouquet of sumptuous Burgundy flavor.

I made it back to *chez Marion* just in time to volunteer myself for the setting of the table. In the country, just as in the city, setting the table is no casual affair. Aside from predicting the superfluous number of plates each person will utilize within the length of one meal, there is the additional memory game of recalling which napkin ring belongs to which person. At Alex and Estelle's we wipe our hands and mouths on the same cloth napkins until they're ready for a good wash. I had always been hesitant to touch my mouth to whichever napkin from the identical white collection I was given, wondering whose mouth it had touched before mine. But at *chez Marion*, Mamie solved the problem by using an assortment of napkin rings, each uniquely assigned to the appropriate person. Léonie used the wooden napkin ring with "Estelle" etched into it, *bien sûr*, fitting as it was. She was proper, beautiful, prim and well-mannered, just like her mother. I wondered if Estelle used that very one every meal that she ate while growing up in the Chanson château across the street. Madame et Monsieur used the pretty silver cuff-like napkin rings with "Hermès Paris" engraved into them (yes, Hermès). But I had not yet managed to memorize the rest, and there would surely be discussion of it when the group convened together *à table*.

We dined on a steamy hot pot of roast chicken and garlic, cooked together with whole round potatoes and chunky pieces of carrot. The lights were off in the dining room while we ate, leaving only the muted white light of a cloud-covered sun to brighten our meal. I couldn't think of a better meal than roast chicken and garlic to comfort the soul and warm the bones at Mamie's on such a rainy, drizzly day. Surprsingly, I didn't care for the bread at *chez Marion*. The *pain du campagne* had a dense, wheaty inside and soft outer crust that was nothing like the crunchy on the outside, fluffy on the inside *rétrodor* I had come to crave. The kids agreed with me, but were forced to eat their rounds as Mamie would not abide it if even one scrap on their plates went uneaten. She used the leftover rounds to soak any sauce from the salad, or juice from the chicken, or lone peas rolling on the plate, and fed the kids their remnants till their plates gleamed white again.

As the kids and Mamie began clearing the table, Monsieur Marion gave me an education on the region—his wine, the weather, tending a vineyard, and then more on the weather. He rattled off all of the necessary aspects of wine-making, referencing good and bad seasons from the early seventies through the present. I listened carefully, smiling and nodding and understanding only bits and pieces as he warbled on in slow and articulate French. His passionate expression and kind conversation were contagious. He regularly remembered what years were too dry and too hot, speaking of 2003 often. Realizing the difficulties of a life so dependent on what is so undependable, I began to understand as I never had before why there is such utter respect and appreciation for one bottle of fine wine. The laborer, the owner, the cultivator—he knows he owes that bottle humble gratitude. He spends his whole life at the mercy of the land, bowing to and toiling against the ground he walks. As the monsieur spoke, I wondered whether he missed it, but I had not the courage to ask him. Once he'd finished his fascinating monologue, I contributed with a final *"merci,"* and I hoped he knew I was thanking him for such an education on his country and the heart and soul behind it.

We three adults convened in the sitting room for an after-lunch café and chocolate while the kids dispersed to the playroom. I was unsure of whether or not I was off-duty, but then Mamie gestured for me to follow her into the ornate, early nineteenth century sitting room where the monsieur sat reading *Le Figaro.* As with Mounie *et* Mip, again the grandparents assumed when I said "journalism major" that I was now a hard news journalist who keeps abreast of every major political issue worldwide. When I named my most recent employer as one of America's top ten newspapers, this did not dissuade them. All of a sudden I had a copy of *Le Figaro* in my lap and a hot demitasse of espresso, freshly brewed from the madame's French press, while Monsieur quizzed me as if I were Diane Sawyer.

Ugh.

Did "journalism" mean "hard news" to everyone who heard the term? I hated hard news. I knew nothing about it. I wanted to be a features writer—human interest, stuff that mattered, stories about people's lives, not cold, hard facts. I loved writing, it was reporting I didn't like. The madame smoked skinny cigarettes and read her own ladies' journals and home décor catalogues while the monsieur questioned me. He was beyond hospitable, forgiving me, if not teaching me, sentence by sentence as I butchered his language in an effort to establish conversation. Monsieur Marion had pegged me as a reporter, whether or not it made sense to either of us. I wasn't sure I believed that he believed I could ever be a reporter, but I obliged him as well as I could and tried to insert the appropriate amount of excitement into my voice as I talked about my career change. But the more I talked, the more I wanted to ask him questions about Chanson, about growing up with Chanson, about Estelle when she was younger, about life. Oh, I could never be a reporter. Quickly, I surrendered to my old tricks, smiling and nodding so much I was sure the movement of my head was hypnotizing us both into slumber.

The day passed, long and slow and enjoyable. There was so much to learn from the monsieur, a native Bourgognian, *et* madame, Bourgognian since she married. I strained to do so by observing them and teaching myself from their conversation. But most of the day I sat reading in the sitting room, scouring the epicurean delights of France, region by region, in a book lent me by the monsieur, and listening with one ear at all times for any sounds of discord echoing up the stairs from the playroom.

It seemed opulent to eat again at dinnertime, but I didn't dare suggest skipping a meal. And the wine, of course, I could never oppose.

I woke the next morning with mounds of small bumps all over my face and throat. I was either allergic to the country or I was getting cabin fever from not taking the long evening walks I had grown accustomed to in Paris. I couldn't have had two more hospitable hosts, but uncertain of my duties and encased by stone walls and an electronic gate, I'd have felt slightly out of line requesting the key and remote control it would take for me to leave the house unaccompanied just for an evening walk. And so I spent most nights inside.

I examined myself in the mirror and I could've sworn my nose looked not only redder, but more bulbous than it had the day before. Was I turning into a Frenchman? And then it occurred to me—the wine. Maybe I was allergic to the wine! Were all Frenchmen with flushed cheeks and red-veined bulbous noses allergic to their own wine without knowing it? I had no idea how to tell my wonderful hosts they had poisoned me. So I went upstairs for breakfast hoping they would not notice the change in my appearance, as they had not noticed their own.

No such luck, though. When I walked into the kitchen,

Mamie looked at me, aghast. *"Qu'est-ce qui se passé?!"* she said, looking at me expectantly for an explanation. I pondered for a brief moment how I would explain to her *en français* that I was allergic to her and her husband's wine, and that it was possible that her husband was just as allergic. Perhaps he took some sort of antibiotic for his ailment, and perhaps I could continue doing the same throughout my visit. But this was a lot of explaining to do on my limited vocabulary. So I settled on a phrase that told her how many glasses of red wine I'd had the day before, telling her that five was a high number for me and perhaps I should not take any today.

She stood there, looking confused, and then hollered "Philippe?!" in a tone so serious I almost expected her next words to be "Call 911."

The monsieur entered the kitchen and examined my splotched face with sincere pity. I blushed, if it was even possible for my face to redden more. Then he turned to his wife, and with tilted heads and furrowed brows, they began a rather heated conversation on either my behalf, or more likely, on behalf of the Burgundy production of wine *en generale*. There were a lot of *"bah ouis"* going on with more hand gestures and wrist flicks than usual. I stood half invisible, half humiliated, awaiting a diagnosis. Once they'd finished, the monsieur turned to me and proclaimed, *"C'est normale."* *Normal*, he'd said. I was turning into a country Frenchman and this was considered normal. He reinforced his prognosis by making sure I had neither fever nor other symptoms and then reassured me once again, *"Oui, c'est normale."* Then he left the kitchen to take the kids with him to morning mass.

The madame shrugged, pursed her lips in question, and then went about her kitchen duties. She was supposedly taking me to tour the town ramparts while the others were at church. I wasn't clear on what time we would leave, exactly what it was we were doing, nor what I needed to do before we left, so I stood in her kitchen with my splotchy face until she turned to me and said, *"Vous êtes prêts?"*

I was ready, though I would have liked a sack to put over my face. We left the house on foot for a walk to the *centre ville* again where a crowd of tourists with local guide assembled. Madame Marion knew the guide and chatted with him briefly till he commenced the tour with an introductory history of Beaune. I realized immediately that this tour would be conducted entirely in French. If I had a difficult time conversing with the cousins from Bergerac, I might as well tune out this guy from the start, who was already deep into the progression and ramifications of the French Revolution. I followed the crowd along the gravel and stones atop the town's ramparts, a little slower than the rest, as I'd chosen my open-toed kitten heels for the excursion. I was sorry I had worn them, but I had done so remembering Mamie's shoes from the day of my arrival. When I glanced at her feet that morning, I noticed she was wearing flats for the first time.

There was an easy sophistication about Madame Marion that, despite her age, made her seem younger and even more beautiful. She was sort of the no-fuss, brush-your-hands-together, a-pinch-of-this-and-that type who confuses girls like me who try so hard to find themselves. She was smart, practical, and alert—all qualities I have never possessed, and I didn't need the shoe lesson to know it. I was reminded of Estelle in the way she walked, the brisk turn of her head when her name was called, and in her suave maneuvering as she moved about the house with the children, and even as she toured with pressing interest the town in which she has resided for the past forty or so years.

That evening, Madame Marion invited me to join her for a piano concert in the nearby town of La Rochepot, while *grand-père* took the kids to the neighbor's swimming pool. Wanting nothing to do with a bathing suit and being quite a lover of classical music, I gladly accepted her generous invitation.

In no time at all, we were driving on the famous road that stretches from one vineyard to the next all the way from Beaune into the Rhone valley wines. Tiny wooden signs marked each town, all of which seemed so humble for the amount of publicity they receive monthly in my *Food & Wine* magazine at home. As we drove out of Beaune, the road became a valley and the land sloped upward on either side. Perfect stripes of green lined the hillsides, row after row. I had gone from never having seen a vineyard to seeing some of the best in the world. *Les vignobles* fascinated me, not only as simply beautiful land, but as true works of art. There was no mistaking that before me lay centuries of tedious, strenuous, incessant labor. Though I had nothing to compare it to and no education on the matter, I couldn't help but see it as a marriage between earth and man. The man must give his utmost faithfully, daily. But he works knowing he is at the mercy of the Creator. The earth bears fruit—a product of soil, sun, rain, wind, and lastly, the labor of man. I had taken no wine at lunch or dinner in fear of turning a deeper shade of Burgundy, but there was no mistaking the beauty, the alluring mystery, the timeless fruit of the country that produced a drink so alive and full of the earth. I sighed, as I would have to be inhuman to truly be allergic to such a wonderful thing. Fortunately for me, my mumps had begun to subside.

We arrived in La Rochepot and Madame, exhibiting yet another youthful quality, parked a few blocks from the church where the concert was being held by yanking the car in reverse and planting it half on the curb in two swift movements. She popped out of the car, and I followed more slowly of course because one of us had to be the grandmother. Outside the church, bundles of families and couples gathered for the concert. The church, which was probably built for this tiny dot of a farm town in the seventeenth century, was humble in size and design, though much more charming than the the churches of America. After the madame graciously paid our way, we took our seats inside on narrow wooden benches so primitive and uncomfortable that I was beginning to believe my seventeenth century building estimate was accurate and that the benches were the originals.

The concert began, and the thunderous pounding of piano keys filled the high-beamed ceiling of the church. I became lost in the music, and let my eyes wander to the church rafters. And there, I spotted a bird. The music poured on and as the bird nervously flitted round and round in circles, I suddenly felt beyond the setting of a piano concert in a French church where an audience was crammed onto wooden benches. I wasn't uninterested but entranced, though I found myself stifling many yawns so as not to offend the madame on my right.

We drove home in silence, both of us drawn into ourselves after the evening's languid serenade. I stared once again out the window as we passed the world-renowned vineyards, wishing I could stand in one while the sun set before us.

To my delight, Monday morning was not much different from the weekend at *chez Marion*. The only differences I noted immediately were the lack of fresh bread and the addition of a housekeeper who was busily setting out breakfast like Mamie had done over the weekend. Actually, I didn't realize she was the housekeeper at the time, so when she greeted me with a friendly smile and a *"Bonjour,"* I thought it only proper to assist her with the breakfast plates. Wrong move, of course, as she took her duties seriously, and wanted no one infringing on them. She shook her head and swatted me away in that pesky French way I'd grown accustomed to, considered cordial in France but hilariously rude in any other country. So instead, I took my place at the breakfast table while she poured my French pressed coffee. I felt suddenly out of place. Even though I was where I was supposed to be and doing what I was supposed to do, none of the things I was doing were remotely relative to the position of an au pair.

The five kids stumbled in with sleepy eyes shortly thereafter, some dressed, some still in pajamas. I made it my immediate task to serve them breakfast before housekeeper or grandmother could remove me from my position. I was still uncomfortable that no instructions were given, so I made whatever obvious efforts I could manage, pouring milk and Nesquik and spreading a soupy, milky pale yellow honey on stale *tartins*. Before I could wipe spilled honey, the housekeeper rubbed the table with a wet rag. Mamie collected breakfast goods and returned them to their appropriate shelved, refrigerated, or countertop spots. I watched the two busy bees. The kids sat there gobbling, making a mess, and having a ball of a time, as usual, while I sat helpless in the face of the professional housekeeping skills around me. I felt completely intimidated and completely unneeded. What good was a nanny in a situation like this? I couldn't understand what they were saying, and I was unsure of what to do (or not to do) so I mustered the strength to ask Monsieur Marion, who sat in his living room reading, for a house key. If I wasn't needed at the house, I was going for a walk.

The monsieur had warned me we might be taking a day trip shortly after breakfast, but I ventured into town for a few minutes anyway. I just needed to check my e-mail—my link to the real world, or at least to one where I was fluent and a functioning member of society. Perhaps a certain acceptance letter had come. I wanted it to be good news because I couldn't stand rejection. To me, rejection of any kind is the most shameful, battering feeling of all. I didn't want to be rejected, but I sort of wanted a reason to deny the acceptance. I was hoping for financial restrictions, or maybe it was too late to register. Maybe I could defer one semester. I wasn't so sure

I was ready for grad school. I wasn't so sure it was the right thing.

But there were no e-mails from my mom. I would have to wait. More time to think couldn't be too bad a thing, could it?

We spent the day at the neighbor's pool and I was finally forced to succumb to the cruelties of bathing suit attire. I worried on the way to the house that I would be pressured to sunbathe topless, as it was *très normale*, especially in these remote parts. And in the not-so-remote parts, *c'est normale* to embrace topless *and* bottomless tanning. Mamie wore a bikini skimpier than one I've ever owned, though I couldn't complain. At least she was wearing one.

Lunch was taken on the patio in picnic style, as well as *goûter*, which Mamie had brought in her insulated sac. And this was the style of summertime at Mamie's. Dinners were light and fresh and taken at home. We ate often on the patio where our skin cooled with the breeze after the day of sun. Wine was poured in abundance, more chilled white than red the hotter and longer the days were in the sun.

On a rainier day, I was performing "puppet show" with Constantin in the clubhouse when I heard him say something about what he "can do" at his Aunt Mireille's. This was a new name to me in the line of Marion-Vladesco relatives, so I asked him to clarify.

"Tante Mireille!" Constantin sang, providing me no further clarification, but at least confirming his sincere like for the person, which is oftentimes more important. Auguste

piped in from the other side of the marionette, echoing Constantin in a chant for Tante Mireille. Still confused and slightly curious why I was just now hearing the name of this famous aunt, I prodded.

"You see her often?" I asked, slipping into elementary French in case Auguste could provide clearer answers.

"Demain!" they both chimed at once. So I assumed that Tante Mireille must be coming for a visit soon. This gave me no reason for alarm until I met Léonie, Jeanne, and Joseph at the bottom of the clubhouse where they were packing up the items from the fort they had made and kept in the garden outside.

"Léonie, why are you guys taking down the fort?" I asked, a little sad to see the nostalgic reminder of my own childhood disappear.

"Because we're leaving," she answered.

"We're going home early?" I asked. As far as I knew we had four more days until the departure date printed on our train tickets.

"No," she said. "We're going to stay at my Aunt Mireille's. Mummy's aunt." I knew it was very likely that Madame and/or the monsieur had informed me of this trip, and that when they did I was practicing my smile and nod routine but hadn't processed a word they'd said. So I gathered my wits and went inside to begin firing away to the madame, in broken French, questions about Aunt Mireille, where she lives, what I should pack, and when we would leave.

Melay, France, is the hometown of the madame and

her sister, Mireille, and where Mireille—Tante Mireille—lives with her husband, Michel. I was not clear on the length of stay, but assumed it would be no more than one night considering we would be going back to Paris shortly after, and I packed my bags once again for the next leg of my *campagne* experience. We left in the early morning, and the farther we drove away from Beaune, the more removed and disoriented I felt. Less and less often was English spoken, less and less was my understanding of my purpose in being here, and I had less and less time to escape even for an hour-long walk. I was completely unneeded but completely unable to leave all the same. Boredom and homesickness were creeping in.

Chapitre Dix

W e arrived in Melay and almost immediately I had a new
word to add to my French vocabulary: *les mouches.*
Flies were everywhere in the *campagne.* They were at the dinner table, on the food, on the walls of the bedroom, and of
course, buzzing over the *toilette.* I thought that Beaune was
the country, but I was wrong. Beaune was more of a city centered amid the French countryside. Melay, on the other hand,
was true *campagne.* It was so far removed from civilization
that the road into town was not paved at all, but beaten down
to a well-trodden dirt path that parts two fields. The two
fields were relatively empty save a few cattle and their waste,
all of which baked in the sun ruthlessly.

Tante Mireille was genial and warm in every way. So
was her daughter, Anne-Laure, who came complete with husband and two kids: Tanguay and Geoffroy. As all of the kids
ran around the front yard, I stood in the front drive, letting it
sink in: I was now the nanny of seven—count them—seven
children, two of whose names I couldn't even pronounce.
Uncle Michel, comical, light-hearted, and dark-skinned,
showed me to my room while I tried to recover from my new

nannying news. Michel led me up the stairs of a guest house he'd recently built, complete with electricity and plumbing. It was unfinished, but an impressive two-story development at any rate.

He was going on about sheet rock or some other material in carpentry when he walked me into my room, which was filled, from one wall to the other, with a row of single beds—five in all. Before I could ask any questions, Léonie, Jeanne, Tanguay, and Joseph filed in behind us, setting suitcases on beds and claiming girl versus boy territory in the room. I held back tears of frustration, thanked Michel with a smile, and walked to the other side of the room where the fifth single bed sat, unclaimed. The kids were out of the room before I even reached the bed. I collapsed facedown, accompanied by a few buzzing flies, and reached under the covers to grab the pillow. I patted around a second, felt nothing but mattress, then lifted my head to look for the pillow. There was no pillow. I glanced down the row of beds—no pillow on any of those, either. I held back my tears, saying to myself, *It's just one night, Rachel. You can handle this. It's no big deal. Just get through this, and before you know it, you'll be back in Paris.* Shortly after my return to Paris, my sister Sarah would be there for a visit. Then together, we would go back home. I sat in the primitive attic room and held on to that thought as tightly as I could.

I wasn't able to summon the courage to leave the room until lunchtime. But I finally ventured downstairs and back into the main house, hoping to assist Anne-Laure with the lunchtime fare. I walked into the kitchen to find casseroles

Rachel Spencer

in the oven, a pot of beans on the stove (where flies swarmed furiously), and a bowl of what appeared to be crepe batter sitting out on the counter. The door from the kitchen to the backyard was wide open, as were all the windows and doors in view. The flies, I supposed, were welcome guests. My skin crawled at the thought of swarms of flies in every room and I fled out the kitchen door in a slight panic. It was much cooler outside than inside and the entire adult crew lay out by the pool watching the kids play in the water. I was by no means comfortable suiting up in front of this crowd and was just about to announce I'd be in the house, when Anne-Laure stood to walk inside. She was topless. I did my best to keep a straight expression, but had completely forgotten what I was about to say. Then her father, Michel, walked from around the house toward her.

"*Bonjour, Papa!*" the topless, thirty-something woman called to her father.

"*Bonjour,*" he said in a cheery tone, stopping to swivel heads and kiss her cheeks.

I was stunned.

Growing up, I used to hide my bras in between stacks of clothes during laundry cycles, and I would scorn my mother if I saw one in open view. It was enough humiliation to know she washed them, and I considered it no business of any other family member to know that I wore them. Since adolescence, I've abandoned some of my prudish practices, but I still feel certain that by the time I'm thirty, I will not have progressed to Anne-Laure's level of confidence, bearing my breasts *en plein-air* to mother, father, aunt, uncle, nieces, nephews, and children. I retreated again to my room, not caring if my help was required for lunch. I'd decided, if possible, that I would hide out in the kids' room until we left for Beaune.

I surfaced for lunch and then again for dinner, trying not to cry every time I came in sight of any of the adults. It was uncertain what they expected of me, though more clear what they thought of me as I was placed at a separate table with the children during mealtimes. Honestly, I was grateful to not have to force conversation or pretend to eat foods for which I had absolutely no appetite. I ate ice cream with the kids for dessert and felt a newfound alliance with them, my confidants and constant companions.

Going to bed that night, though hard-earned, was less than relaxing. There was an unpleasant odor in and around my bed, one that smelled curiously like urine. I tried to tell myself it was just the scent of new pine from Michel's construction, but I worried that the sheets on my bed had not been changed since the children's last visit. To make matters worse, the sheets were damp. The air outside sat hot and heavy, and air-conditioning was a foreign if not unknown thought at this place in Melay. For at least an hour I tried to erase thoughts of urine-stained sheets from my head, in between issuing loud, exasperated "shhhhhs" every five minutes to quiet the kids' muffled giggles and murmurings. I listened to the lullaby of nearby flies, and prayed for morning to come quickly.

When I awoke the next day with disheveled hair, wet pajamas, sunken eyes, and an aching back, the other beds were already empty. I dressed quickly, all thoughts of appearing stylish completely abandoned. There was no way I would make it through the day without washing my hair. I decided to eat breakfast and then take refuge in the shower. Grumbling, I climbed down the wooden steps into the main house. There was immediate heat beaming from the sky, baking the brick and dirt grounds of the house. No relief. I met the group at the patio table outside for breakfast, where the coffee was not the rich brew of Mamie's French press, but instant grounds dissolved in boiling water. Sacrilege. I mourned the loss and dreamed of the high-tech espresso machine back in the Vladesco house in Paris. The kids gobbled *tartins* slathered with syrupy honey while I sat in the sun and stewed. I was sure I couldn't stand the discomfort of another day in the country, drinking instant coffee from a bowl, as if mugs were a highly valued commodity or too formal for the breakfast setting.

To avoid screaming in a burst of utter irritation, I locked myself in the bathroom to take my shower. It felt like days since I'd had one. I depended on it, even at this early hour, to give me a half hour of much needed freedom from the kids and to wash away the events of the past twenty-four hours. I felt overtaken by an alien mood of cruel and evil intent, cursing nearly everything I saw. I hated this place, but I would love the shower.

This of course proved my naivete. There was no shower. There was just a claw-foot bathtub—the kind that any other time would have looked charming. I guess I should have been grateful for the slight update to its antiquated design, but I wasn't. So I cursed the damn handheld shower hose attached to the faucet. Whatever, I was desperate. I stripped off my clothes that were already wet with sweat—either from the heat or my temper—and started the water. Ice cold. *Dammit.* I couldn't cuss enough. I don't cuss, though, do I?

Then seconds later . . . *bzzzz.* Damn flies. Damn flies and damn breasts everywhere in this place. My skin crawled at the thought; I've never felt so uncomfortable in my life. By that point, I was mad enough to ignore the fact that the water was freezing cold. I climbed into the tub, wondering how on earth anyone could wash hair adequately under such a miserable drip. I was leaning backward against the porcelain, contorting my body to maneuver the handheld hose over my head while using the other hand to shake water through my hair when I heard noises at the door. I froze.

You have got *to be kidding me.*

Someone knocked, and before I could even shout, *"I'm in here!"* the three youngest boys ran straight through the bathroom, hollering and chanting, to a door on the opposite side of the room and flung it open as if to use it. Then they discarded it and ran back across the bathroom to the main door, which connected to the hallway. I yelped in humiliation but they paid me no mind, disappearing once again and screaming more nonsense as they went—leaving both doors wide open. Apparently the locks were decorative.

After my makeshift shower, which proved more stressful than beneficial, Anne-Laure appeared, looking grimly toward me from the hallway. I guessed she had heard me screaming at the boys who denied me privacy.

"How was your shower?" she asked.

"Not much of one," I said. "I guess I didn't lock the bathroom doors!"

"It was only Geoffroy," Anne-Laure said.

I narrowed my eyes and looked at her, making no attempt to smile, which is how I usually excuse myself from unwanted conversation. I didn't understand how her statement was any sort of justification. In fact, it wasn't even relevant. Whether it was "just Geoffroy" had nothing to do with the fact that I still hadn't had five minutes alone. It wasn't "just Geoffroy," by the way. It was Geoffroy, Auguste, and Constantin screaming at the top of their lungs. Why did they get to scream and I didn't? And now, I wanted to scream louder than ever.

In the late afternoon, when the sun grew too hot, the adults called the children out of the pool in exchange for a bike ride or indoor play. Secretly, I wondered if the real reason for this was that the parents wanted their "adult swim." But I stopped myself before more nude images soiled my mind, volunteering instead to accompany the kids on their bike ride. At least it would get me away from the house.

We left, the oldest four and I, to journey the unpaved road beyond the sign that read MELAY and beyond the cows loitering in the fields. Constantin, Auguste, and Geoffroy stood whining in the front drive as we wheeled away. I felt bad, but I knew they were too young to keep pace with the older bunch. I promised Constantin I would take him for a ride, just the two of us, when I returned. Rarely have I fully appreciated the freeing sensation of wind against my face as I did that day, riding at full speed along the country road. The sound of the wind in my ears was equally therapeutic—no children laughing, crying, whining, arguing, talking, breathing, nothing. No nonsensical French chitchat itching my ears. No sounds, no restrictions, just wind.

It was also the first time I'd gotten exercise in many days. Since coming to Beaune, all of the benefits of my daily Parisian walks had been reversed by the feasting and relaxing at *chez Marion*. I peddled harder, breathing easier, feeling strongly renewed. I gave thanks to God for that moment of freedom, that quiet untouched moment. I would never again take for granted the beauty of being alone, free to do what I wanted. My heart welled in gratitude, washing clean the hours and days I had spent frustrated and idle in the country.

Just as we reached the end of the path, there was a loud, quick bang. I hopped off my bike, ready to jump into action. Before I could determine the cause, another shot rang through the air. I left my bike and jogged up the path to meet the kids, who were gathered around Joseph, laughing. Nearing the scene, I saw his bike tumbled over to one side on the ground, both tires hopelessly busted and deflated. The kids thought this was hilarious, and made their own bursting nooses followed by loud laughter, using the word *"explosé"* to describe the debilitated state of Joseph's bike. I shooed them on their way, instructing Léonie to lead them straight home to explain what happened to Tante Mireille and Mamie.

After the others sped ahead and faded from view, Joseph and I picked up his bike and mine, and slowly made our way down the travel road toward home. We walked in silence, and I attempted to wheel both Joseph's bike and my own, as Joseph had bloodied knees and palms to contend with and I felt sorry for him. But seeing me struggle, he took his bike, with wheels too battered to roll, and carried it along. He was a good-hearted, well-raised country boy, who did not see fit to have me, a girl, compromise my own comfort on his behalf. We made the bike exchange without words, since I didn't speak French and he didn't speak English, supplementing with sighs and slight chuckles. Since coming to the *campagne*, Joseph had made eye contact with me maybe two or three times at most.

I wasn't sure if he was afraid of me or if he was shy, but I hadn't had the time or energy to attempt to draw him out of his shell. But as we walked along the dirt road, he smiled a polite grateful smile, and I knew this was my chance. I spoke to him in broken French, asking questions about Bergerac and past summers at Mamie's. He answered all politely with one or two words, keeping his eyes on the dirt path, but smiling all the same. As we walked, the sun dozed to our left, hanging low over the unspoiled fields and distant hillsides.

It was my favorite time of day and I told him so, the hour when the sun casts a golden glow over the land and shadows grow long. He told me that the French have a phrase for that time of day: *coucher du soleil*. Translated into English, it means "the sun putting itself to bed." And then he agreed with me that it was the most beautiful time of day.

We made it home and were greeted in the front drive by Monsieurs Marion and Michel, tools in hand, ready to evaluate the "explosion." I left the men to their work and went inside to wash hands and prepare for another dinner with the kids, dreading yet another French country mystery meal and longing for the gourmet of Alex's kitchen. To my surprise, I found my napkin ring at the grown-up table, and so I took my place between Monsieur Marion and Tante Mireille.

There were several courses for the adults. The kids though, ate in one course, finishing quickly in order to present for the adults a dinner theatre, so to speak, written and directed by Mademoiselle Léonie Vladesco. Not knowing there would be an admission fee, I borrowed a centime from Michel (who passed them to all adults at the table) to place in the bucket Jeanne carried around the table. I relaxed considerably, one might say, after more glasses of wine than I could count, and felt neither an ounce of guilt nor inappropriateness for it. And if I turned into an old French man, I would at least die a happy one! We watched and clapped and cheered, until the sky was too black to observe the darting children in the yard.

I fell into bed with relief, too intoxicated to care about the urine smell or the buzzing flies, and thrilled at the promise of returning to Chez Marion the next day. I dozed off to sleep before I could count the hours until morning.

Rachel Spencer

* * *

I had forgotten how good air-conditioning felt on a sticky, sweaty hot face. I sat in the front seat of the car with the monsieur and aimed the jets directly toward me. The three boys sat in the back, uncharacteristically quiet, as we headed home toward Beaune. I turned around to check on them, and saw that they were all awake but with drooping eyes and tired faces. They were exhausted after hours and days of hard play in the country. We sputtered along slowly, discussing weather and politics, while Mamie drove separately with the girls in her car, speeding dangerously along the *autoroute*.

Being in the country—the real wild-animal, fly-plagued, plumbing-deficient French country—was the most sobering French experience I'd had thus far. In fact, I was so sober that I would never feel the need to return under such dire circumstances—I would never again describe such antiquated methods of bathing as "quaint," nor would I call the ways of the inhabitants "charming." I, who once professed to friends and relatives that I was born two centuries too late, was finally grateful for having been born at the time I was. I made a vow to return to Paris with an immense gratitude for all of the amenities of modern life. In my post–French country days, I would buy any fancy electronic gadget that was thrust at my face—just as long as it did things more quickly, was fly-free, and came with air-conditioning. *Au revoir,* French country.

Sure, I appreciated the educational aspect of seeing other regions of France. But I would put this education to use for one purpose and one purpose only: to remind me never to return to such an environment. I was grateful to have visited once in my life so that I would never have to question again whether I was a country girl. No matter how "romantic" country living seemed, now I knew I did not belong there. Regardless, two things were certain. One, even if I wasn't sure whether Paris was a perfect fit for me, I could live there my whole life without wondering ever again whether perhaps I was better suited for country living. And two, it was certain that the only way I would ever return to the country would be if I stayed under the roof of a Michelin-rated five-star bed and breakfast, complete with Jacuzzi tub, wireless internet, and other modern conveniences.

I leaned back in the seat, letting the air conditioning pummel me. In a few days, my sister Sarah was coming to Paris to visit. In my head, I made a list of all the modern, shallow, commercial things we would do when she arrived. I hoped she would share with me an unabashed pride to be an American tourist in Paris. What had I ever felt ashamed of?

I shut my eyes and inhaled, wishing I could open my eyes to Sarah right then. Instead, I opened them, sighed in exhaustion, and prayed silently, half joking and half begging for mercy. *God bless her, my dear sister Sarah. And always, God bless America.*

Once we returned to *chez Marion*, we only had the remainder of the day and the night before catching the train to Paris. The time passed so quickly I never got to ask about visiting the vineyards. There were fabric shops and wine shops and several museums I had wanted to visit as well. I felt foolish to have not once asked to be dismissed from the house to explore the ancient town at my leisure, but then, I wasn't a tourist here. I wasn't sure I was a nanny, but I was certain I wasn't a tourist. The next morning, we said good-bye to Madame at her front door. She smiled tightly but warmly and briskly patted the back of each of her grandchildren as they exited the doorway toward the car where the monsieur waited to chug us along to the train station.

There were parts of Beaune I missed before I even left. I loved saying *"à table!"* three times a day. There was no joy like watching five French children scurry to their grandmother's table, eager to stake claim to their respective serviette. (I didn't correctly remember both the assigned seat and assigned napkin ring of each person until our last dinner there.) Dinnertime, despite my ill attention to Marion family napkin traditions, was my favorite time of all. The kids behaved more sweetly when they came to the table dressed in their pajamas. I knew the day would end soon enough, so I could relish that mealtime hour when everything seemed right and good—the hour when the sun "put itself to bed." I would never forget it.

Most of all, I would miss the monsieur and the books he loaned me, all of which described just a hint of the vineyards, mysterious land on which I never stepped foot. Glancing at them from a distance through the glass of a car window was as close as I came. But I would keep my posters of Le Chateau de la Tour, a treasure from the market, and perhaps make it my goal to visit Beaune again one day. I considered Monsieur Marion the last of the *père et fils* of Chanson. The vineyard and the wine were once his life. But now it was one of many labels lost, under the ownership of Bollinger. Monsieur Marion—and all the fathers and sons before him for 249 years—catalogued every drop of dew in their land. He remembered every year by heart. It was in his blood; it was the air he breathed. During our final dinner in Melay— the night when we all indulged more than usual—Michel brought a dusty green glass bottle of wine to the table. It wasn't labeled, or marked in any way. Michel poured the glass for Monsieur Marion first—a test, I believe it was, to name the year in which the wine had been produced. Monsieur Marion smelled, sipped, and smiled. "1972," he said, not to be stumped by his brother-in-law. At once Michel stepped back in disbelief. He slapped his knee and hollered a loud cheer, applauding Monsieur Marion for his near-flawless skill. It was a 1973 white Burgundy. I was impressed. Impressed that a man could be so attuned to the elements of his work that he could taste a wine and recall which 365 days drew forth such flavor. The wine was a little musty for me, but then again I wasn't alive in 1973. So I trusted it was a gem, as it was described by those with a more acquired taste, *on peut dire.*

I learned from Monsieur Marion that Beaune wines were made mostly, if not all, from Aligoté grapes, or *raisins.* I wondered what the ground would do with any other seed. It seemed after centuries of tradition, the Aligoté and the Beaune earth were one—inseparable as marrow to bone, soul to spirit. Oh, to have tasted and seen all the very good years.

And so I left the Aligoté earth intrigued and humbled and wanting more, feeling I owed it that. But I left the country exhausted enough to welcome Paris back with open arms, the city where maybe I belonged after all, where my sister would help right all that had gone wrong, and where I would usher in my quickly approaching return to America.

Chapitre Onze

I was already standing when the TGV rolled into the Gare de Lyon. Graffiti-covered concrete walls again bordered both sides of the train as we slowed to a stop. Everything outside looked dirty. It was noisy already and the urgency of the city was back. Passengers stood and pushed toward the exit of the train, and I pushed right along with them, anxious to smell that rotten city air outside.

It always took losing something for me to know what I'd missed; it always took leaving to know I wanted to go back. As we stood to disembark the train from the country, I knew I wanted to be back in Paris. My spirit rested. I felt a deep longing fulfilled that warmed me from the inside out. We were home. *Home.* I smiled widely and tapped my foot against the floor, anxious to smell the raw sewage, the rubbish, the dirty walls of graffiti outside. I was light-hearted, almost giddy, and leaked a tiny giggle audible to those closest to me.

Léonie looked up at me like I was crazy. I tried to calm the thrill that rushed through me just so I didn't burst in front of her. I gave her a warm smile and petted her head,

Rachel Spencer

thinking I had masked my excitement. "You seem glad to be home," she said.

"Oh, I am so glad," I gushed, ready to sing the praises of 37, Boulevard Pereire with her. But as my eyes twinkled, Léonie frowned.

"You didn't like it at Mamie's?" she asked.

"Oh, of course I did!" I lied. "I loved it." I petted her head again, hoping that I didn't offend her. She was sticking up for her Mamie, and for her mom, of course.

We exited the train with luggage in tow. Constantin bopped along in between Léonie and me. Léonie was silent and I feared she did not understand. I was just glad to be home. I had never been happier to go home. And now that we were in Paris again, I felt even closer to my real home, the place where I would settle. Arkansas sounded so peaceful compared to the city. It would be peaceful—easy, calm, quiet. I would miss the city, but oh, to be in a place I could call home. So we walked on, and I sucked in all of the dirty, city air I could, knowing my lungs wouldn't stay polluted for long.

When we arrived at the house, we found Alex in the kitchen conducting a grand orchestra of gourmet. Pavarotti's greatest tenor arias blared through the speakers of a new Bang & Olufsen stereo on the shelf. I took the newly purchased high-end electronic device to mean that Estelle was out of town on business. Indeed she was. Alex greeted each of us with warm affection, inspired if not exuberant to see us. I was surprised how glad I was to see him too, like an old friend, a real homecoming, and Alex was creating a homecoming feast.

The kids dropped their luggage in the TV room, and I dropped mine in the hall and the kitchen. Alex didn't care about such things, and rather than unpack, I joined him to watch him cook.

I loved his style of cooking. He tended to sprinkle hors d'oeuvre throughout the kitchen, prone to eat his way through his work. Thinly sliced prosciutto lay on waxed paper on the counter near the sink. A bottle of nectar sat on the breakfast table.

"Did you buy a new juice, Alex?" I asked.

"Uh, what?" Alex said. "Oh, the nectar. Yes. You want to try it? Try it." He said the word *nectar* like it was French, not English. I loved that about Alex. *Nectaire*, he pronounced it, with a thrust in the guttural *r* sound. He was always giving a French accent to English words, and I wondered if he was partly to blame for my own misunderstood Franglais. Because of Alex, I wanted every word I spoke to sound French.

He poured me a glass and I drank it. It wasn't as light and clean as the pear one I'd tried a few weeks ago. This one was heavier and sweeter, a berry nectar. He watched my face as I drank.

"You don't like it?" Alex asked.

"Oh," I said. It wasn't an answer, but he went on before I could finish.

"Would you rather have champagne? Why don't we have some champagne," Alex said, again not waiting for my answer. "Léonie!" Alex yelled. *"Viens, s'il-te-plaît!"*

Léonie entered the kitchen running, out of breath from bolting down the three flights of stairs. No doubt she'd been on the computer, of which she had been deprived the past ten days. Alex ordered her to fetch a bottle of champagne for us. I felt slightly guilty, knowing this was usually my chore. But then again, I felt slightly more grown-up now than I had a few weeks ago. Tonight, home alone with him and the kids, perhaps I felt slightly more his dinner date. I wasn't the kid or even the nanny running to the cellar to fetch the wine. I wasn't finishing last-minute chores or setting the table. I was lounging in the kitchen with Alex, enjoying his company. And if I wasn't mistaken, he was enjoying mine. My defenses were down. I'd been away ten days and was terribly homesick. I was exhausted. I was glad to be home. Whatever I felt, I was glad to embrace it. Whatever I felt, it was good compared to the last ten days—to every day in the last few weeks, actually. Dinner date or not, I felt pampered and indulgent as I anticipated my first sip of champagne.

When Léonie brought the bottle, we tore pieces of prosciutto and filled glasses with champagne, eating every last morsel and drinking every last drop. *J'adore la champagne.* There were other small bites of food strewn across the counter and I felt at ease to help myself to whatever pleased me. I usually knew that I would not like something whenever Alex introduced it with superlatives, but I felt bold that night. *Normalement*, if he said, "You have to try this—this is *fantastique*," I detested it. Alex was, after all, the quintessential Frenchman who liked his meat raw, his cheese completely spoiled, and his hors d'oeuvres from parts of animals I considered waste. *Normalement*, I was as American as they came, and no one could tell me it was American to eat meat that hadn't been cooked or cheese that hadn't been pasteurized or appetizers that weren't fried. Perhaps tonight, though, I wasn't so *typique*. I felt, *en effet, une petite française*, and the mystery associated with French women revealed a little of itself to me.

I sampled the *crème de la crème* of precursors, which truly were *fantastique*, and only whetted my appetite for our dinner feast. I laughed with and laughed at Alex as I watched him slice and dice to *La donna è mobile*. Alex may have been a great chef, but he was not a tidy one. He cut with force, causing whole chunks of vegetable to fly into the air. Oils splattered as he poured and stirred together a mix of liquids for the meat marinade. With his combination of grand movements and the blare of the opera, he made the kitchen his stage like a conductor facing his symphony orchestra. I imagined him dressed in a formal tuxedo, coattails flying, arms waving furiously, whisking beads of sweat from his furrowed brow in rhythm with the music.

"Voilà!" Alex said. He finished chopping and asked me to prepare the sauce. I kept myself from bursting into operatic serenades and, under the eye of the maestro, concocted a sauce, which Alex pronounced "sosse," for our salad.

At nine o'clock, dinner was ready. Under Alex's direction, Constantin screamed up the staircase at the top of his lungs, "*À table!*" to his sister. Then, not as shy as I was to embrace operatic fervor, he marched into the kitchen humming bars of *Recondita Armonia*.

We ate *bavette*, which Alex assured me was a beautiful cut of beef that the butcher specifically chose for him.

"*Bavette*—I mean, it is only for special occasions,

Rachel Spencer

okay?" Alex said. "And just try it like this—*au barbecue*—you didn't eat like this in Beaune."

Of course I smiled—and even cooed—as he boasted that the *boucherie* would go out of business if it weren't for his faithful patronage. So of course the butcher always chose special cuts of meat for Alex. Of course the butcher would hack right through a gorgeous hunk of meat just to slice the perfect cuts for Alex. Of course. *Bien sûr.* But in my champagne-blitzed state, I wanted to believe him. I even supposed this really was a special occasion. With only four of us at the table, I felt more relaxed than I could remember feeling all ten days in Beaune. No formalities, no nervousness in my manners. And Alex was right, we did *not* eat like this in Beaune. There was nothing like this in Beaune.

The kids ate quickly and departed for parts unknown in the house, but Alex and I lingered at the table, enjoying the muted sounds of Pavarotti pouring through the open sliding glass door from the kitchen into the garden air. I had an inkling Alex's musical selection for the evening hinted at his anticipation of the family vacation to the Amalfi coast. Next to the bottle of nectar on the kitchen table, I noted a *Fodor's Guide to Naples, Capri, and the Amalfi Coast* stacked on top of *Italy for the Gourmet Traveler.* I knew he was getting antsy. I would be too if I were part of a culture that regularly withdrew for month-long vacations. Apparently all of Paris shuts down in August. Most of them packed up for Provence and the Riviera; Alex & Co., however, travel worldwide. Last year they took an African safari and the year before, they rented a yacht and sailed around the Grecian islands. I was impressed to learn that Alex was such a seasoned sailor, but when I told him so, he corrected me immediately.

"We hired someone—are you crazy?" Alex said. "I wouldn't drive that thing myself!"

By the time Alex and I rose from our places at the patio table, the kids were fast asleep. He invited me to listen to music with him in the museum of a living room, where the sound system compared to that of a recording studio. ("The sound is amazing," he said. "You've never heard anything like it.") What amazed me about French men was how little they regarded invitations like the one Alex gave me. "Oh, come into my living room. Sit on the sofa with me. Listen to Mozart—or do you like Beethoven? Have you ever heard more beautiful sounds? Close your eyes—you'll enjoy it better. I'll drink my brandy and puff a two-hundred-dollar cigar. Just sit with me." Alex thought nothing of this, because it meant nothing to him. On nights past, even Estelle watched Alex invite me, without so much as a blink of an eye. So without a second thought, I had joined him previously. But I hadn't felt so much like his dinner date then. I had felt like the American nanny to whom he was kind to extend such a cultural, educational experience. But Estelle wasn't watching, and I'd sipped too much champagne. That night, I was way too attracted to that crazy, dangerous Frenchman to do anything but fake a yawn and decline his invitation.

In the middle of the night, I woke to use the toilet. I'd had one too many glasses of wine and champagne, and it was my third trip since I'd gone to bed. I had fallen asleep in my clothes but after the first trip to the bathroom, I stripped off my pants and belt, leaving on just my white button-down oxford. I stumbled toward the toilet that was just outside the nanny room in the basement hallway. My eyes were half shut when, as I rounded the corner, I bumped into Alex. We stood, face to face. I immediately dropped my head and cleared my throat.

"Oh. Ooh. Sorry," Alex said.

Though my eyes weren't open completely, I swear I saw him look me up and down. He stood there in front of me, looking at me, but I stared at the ground. This was not as easily avoidable as the living room music invitation had been.

In the bathroom I saw that the hours of tossing and turning in bed had caused most of the buttons on my shirt to open. Worse, there was no denying the red satin underwear I wore underneath. I bit my lip and knew I should've been horrified, but truth be told, I took a second glance in the mirror. It wasn't like I was staring at him, for crying out loud. I was just staring at myself in the mirror, replaying in my mind how he had stared at me.

But that was as far as it could go, and even that was shameful. Adultery is a sin. I was an adulteress! What was I thinking?! But really, this was silly. Just like that hound never thought twice about inviting foreign young girls into his den, he had probably already fumbled upstairs and gone to bed without so much as a second thought. He'd seen more in his life. Good grief, he was married to a French woman. I remembered even Sarah told me Alex once saw her in her silk pajama boxers. I was certain red satin underwear was worse than silk pajama boxers, but *c'est la vie.* He was gone when I came out to go back to bed, just as I'd suspected. So I decided that in the morning, I would pretend the whole episode never happened.

I didn't see Alex the next morning, much to my relief.

To cleanse my conscience, I spent the next day with the kids preparing for Sarah's arrival. Sarah knew the city so much better than I, so I decided to wait on all the touristy activities until she arrived. I spent the day cooking, eating, and reading French recipes in Alex's cookbooks. My obsession with the kitchen grew the longer I stayed in it. Mostly I was mesmerized by how Alex cooked with such minimal fuss. He used only the freshest ingredients, but he was in Paris—what other kind of ingredients did he have to choose from? American grocery stores were not so readily supplied. I savored the philosophy of French cuisine—namely summertime cuisine—absorbing all I could until the days came when *courgettes* and *aubergines* once again became foreign produce.

I read recipes and converted grams and milliliters into cups while Constantin and Léonie made drawings and crafts to welcome Sarah. I had forgotten the multiple uses of dried pasta shells, buttons, and clothespins until I peeked at their art stations. I wrote menus for the dinner parties I wanted to host when I moved back to the States. I even planned ahead for a New Year's Eve cocktail and hors d'oeuvre party. Alex owned hundreds of gourmet cookbooks. They inspired me to plan party after party with dozens of different themes and genres of food. Soon I had made seating charts and mock invitations for my "Harvest Welcome" dinner with friends. I missed my friends and I was anxious for Arkansas, as odd as it seemed coming from a girl who sat among the riches of Paris. But Arkansas was home and friends were there, along with my own kitchen and dinner party dishes. As I thought about return-ing there to settle and slow down, I grew tired and a little sad sit-ting in the Vladescos' kitchen. I plotted the various pairings of warm goat cheese salad, onion soup, tomato tart, quiche Lor-raine, garlic roast chicken, *gratin dauphinois*, and various *galettes*, until I grew bored enough that Arkansas seemed still a ways off. Savoring my last days, I shifted back to being an American tourist and planned an itinerary for Sarah's visit.

Sarah's coming tomorrow! The more I said it to myself, the lighter I felt. We had three days together before Léonie and Constantin, with Diane, went to the U.K. for a summer camp. On that same day, Sarah and I were taking a trip to the south of France. When we returned, we would have just two nights and one day in Paris. And so I relinquished my efforts to blend with the chic Parisians and at last embraced the ob-noxious American tourist within myself. It was a wonderful feeling, a deliciously devilish indulgence, and I grimaced in delight as I plotted cliché adventures for two sisters—two au pairs—two Americans in Paris.

> ### *Wednesday*
> *12:00—Sarah arrives.*
> *12:15—Lunch together chez Vladesco:*
> *check nanny book for menu, plus make lemon tart (make today).*
> *3:00—Buy TGV tickets to the South of France.*

> *Run Estelle's errands together.*
>
> *Eat dinner at home. (Sarah to bed early to sleep off jetlag.)*
>
> <u>Thursday</u>
>
> *Sleep late.*
>
> *Make pancakes.*
>
> *Take kids to Le Louvre, Laduree, Notre Dame.*
>
> *Shop on Faubourg Saint-Honore (Chanel and Hermes!!)*
>
> *Take kids to a movie (per Sarah's request in e-mail to me).*
>
> <u>Friday</u>
>
> *Buy souvenirs for friends and family at home.*
>
> *4:00—Diane comes home from Spain.*
>
> *Rent, watch <u>Dirty Dancing</u>.*
>
> *Family dinner.*
>
> <u>Saturday</u>—*Kids leave for the UK; we leave for Antibes.*

Immediately, the most pressing issue jumped out at me. I needed to make a lemon tart for lunch tomorrow. After watching Alex several times, it turned out that the oven was not so scary; it didn't even attack. I rummaged through the recipes I'd brought from home until I found the one for my *mémé*'s lemon meringue pie. Perhaps if I made it without meringue, it would resemble a tart.

The recipe wasn't the hard part—the ingredients were difficult. For all the fresh produce and gourmet sauces available in the Vladescos' kitchen, the basic staples of sugar and flour were impossible to locate.

I summoned the kids to the front door where they led me again to the *monoprix*. No rainstorms this time—there wasn't a cloud in the sky.

At the store, I was bewildered to find a baking aisle stocked full of myriad grains, even flavors of flour and sugar. And in all that abdundance, I found not one sack of flour that resembled the all-purpose, self-rising flour I needed to construct my tart. Nor could I find one sack of sugar that resembled the grainy, crystallized form of Imperial brand granulated sugar. Every bag was specialty flour or sugar—a variety unlike any I'd ever seen, all for the purpose of baking patisseries and breads and fine chocolates, no doubt. I didn't know how to make patisseries and croissants, though. I wanted to make a lemon tart from the same basic recipe as my *mémé*'s lemon meringue pie. But I couldn't, not here. I couldn't bake French food and I couldn't bake mine. So I bought the sacks closest to American staples, took the kids, and went back home.

Needless to say, substituting other ingredients for flour and sugar in a recipe mostly comprised of flour and sugar did not produce prize-winning results. I would have even settled for something that looked plain, but calling it plain was pure flattery. The tart was ugly. The filling was murky, gellish, and oddly bubbly, certainly not the dessert of choice I wanted to present to Sarah tomorrow in celebration of her arrival. So we ate it—Léonie, Constantin and I. The whole thing. I added berries and lemon zest curls to the top to cover up the rather interesting surface, but the kids didn't seem to mind either way. Despite bad ingredients and bad appearance, it tasted amazing. It was pure zesty lemon perfection—sweet and tart at the same time. But after all the trouble I'd gone through baking the tart, it wasn't the taste that amazed me most. After a summer of toil, after fear and rejection, at last I had conquered the oven.

I went to sleep that night feeling so safe, so secure. Sarah would take care of everything from here on out—including me. I didn't have to worry anymore, I didn't have to wonder whether I had done the right thing. I didn't have to stutter in a made-up Franglais language or hide from Alex after dinner. Everything felt easy. I drifted to sleep. It was the last time I slept alone in the nanny bedroom.

The sun shone bright the next morning. I woke the kids for a change, since they woke me most mornings, got them dressed, and we all left the house. It was a morning for a bakery celebration; Sarah was coming today.

Ruddy Cheeks hollered orders and spat in faces with vigor; it was as if she knew today was a more exciting day than usual. The kids chose *pains au chocolat*, I chose a croissant. After all, few days remained of my time in Paris. I thought it best to savor the quintessential Parisian *boulangerie, le croissant*, considering nowhere else on earth made them as well as Ruddy Cheeks and her crew.

We sat on the bench outside the bakery entrance and gobbled our treats. I watched the line grow and curve around the sidewalk. I listened to Ruddy Cheeks yelling orders. Crotchety, crusty Frenchmen walked by with their mangy mutts. Persnickety, preppy Frenchwomen walked by with their toy poodles. The cheese shop on the corner advertised a special discount on Camembert. The produce stand down the street spilled over with a fresh display of melon. The dogs barked. The trash in the street stank. I smelled the medley of aromas and odors, stenches and fragrances, baking together under the warmth of the sun. Paris, as it turned out, was a beautiful thing. But I'd never doubted that—just doubted myself in it.

I bought the day's supply of *rétrodors* and one more *pain au chocolat* before we left the vicinity. Sarah loved *pain au chocolat* and it was the least I could to welcome her. It was mid-morning when we returned home, and not too early to start lunch for Sarah. I was anxious to impress her with my new culinary skills, and to pass the time until her arrival.

The menu for lunch, as written by Estelle in the nanny book, listed lamb chops with potatoes and carrots. I'd make the carrots just as I'd seen Alex do it—with nothing more than a little olive oil and sea salt. And I would add to Estelle's menu a green leaf salad to show Sarah how I'd been trained in making good *sauce*. Alex left Pavarotti in the new flat-surface BeoSound stereo so I turned it on to conduct my own grand orchestra of gourmet. Cooking alone in the spacious Vladesco kitchen, I felt inspired, full of possibility. I covered the lamb with fragrant provencal herbs, loving the aroma and dreaming of my own trip to Provence, just days away. With liberation, I coated each chop in sea salt and crushed pepper. I had dressed in all black for Sarah's grandiose arrival—black flared pants, black sleeveless shell, black strappy stilettos, and I draped a slate blue silk wrap around me for dramatic flair. In the old-money, newspaper-society-pages way, I felt elegant, rich, and famous dressed as I was, listening to opera and cooking lamb.

I started with the carrots, broiling them with olive oil just as I'd seen Alex do. They sizzled until just soft and the oil caramelized on top. Next, I started on a new dessert, one that did not involve flour or sugar. I baked peaches sprinkled with cinnamon and glazed with a maraschino kirsch. I'd bought the peaches fresh from the market the day before. In all my life—even growing up in Texas where Fredericksburg peaches were famous—I had never tasted a peach so succulent or sweet. When the lamb chops were ready, it was twelve noon. Léonie had set the table with care, Constantin sat down with a slice of *rétrodor* in his mouth. I could hardly wait for the buzz at the front door.

By 1 p.m., Constantin and Léonie had eaten all the slices of *rétrodor* I'd set in the breadbasket on the table. Rather than spoil their appetite with more fillers, I served them lunch. I, though, would wait for Sarah. *Where was she?* At 2 p.m. I had cleared the table and the kids' plates. I tried to ignore the hunger pangs in my stomach and felt sad that the lamb, potatoes, and carrots had turned cold and un-appetizing.

The kids retreated to the TV room after much begging, tugging, and questioning in regard to Sarah's arrival. They were almost as anxious as I was for her to come, but not quite. Thinking back to my first day in Paris, I decided we should meet her at the bus stop rather than have her walk home alone. After all, it's a long walk when pulling heavy luggage and the sun is hot. I called the kids to the door and we left the house to wait at the bus stop. I knew exactly which bus she would take because she was the one who'd told me the route when I arrived. We arrived at the bus station just as line 92—the one from l'Étoile—pulled to a stop. I felt strange meeting my sister out in the middle of Paris with two kids, kids she'd first introduced to me. Everything in life, I supposed, really did come full circle. Léonie and Constantin beamed with excitement. I squeezed their hands as we watched passengers climb off the bus.

"I see her!" Constantin shouted.

"That's not her," Léonie said.

"Okay!" Constantin said. He had enough confidence to be wrong and maintain his excitement. He picked out another passenger and pointed. "Is that her?" Léonie rolled her eyes in irritation.

Then I saw Sarah climbing down the back steps of the bus. I knew I had been lonely, but I didn't realize how much until I saw my big sister right there in front of me in Paris. Without motioning to the kids, I ran. There she was. I wasn't alone anymore.

Sarah looked exhausted. She tugged bags off the bus and readjusted her clothes before she noticed me. "What?!" she said.

"We couldn't wait!" I said. "Hey!"

We hugged and I took her luggage and walked on, back toward home, letting her ooh and ahh over how much Constantin and Léonie had grown since she saw them last. The three hugged, Constantin and Léonie fighting for her attention and for her hands to hold. I was glad. They needed someone to be more concerned and attentive than I had been. And I was glad for Sarah. She loved it here so much. So did I, of course, just not in the same way. Sarah's confidence allowed her to travel alone, to adapt to new environments, to not be affected by circumstances. I was still growing my backbone. I wanted to fit, I just didn't know where. Paris was beautiful, everyone knew that. So of course I loved it. Of course I knew I was living out a great opportunity. But I didn't quite believe I deserved it. I felt like a fraud, or like I was trying to be someone like Sarah—someone who knew how to be herself no matter where she went. Except that I couldn't even figure out who I was supposed to be, no matter where I was. But I still tried to create the identity I thought fit Paris best, trying to make it something it wasn't to me. I was trying too hard to be something I wasn't, wishing I could be someone I wasn't. I was still learning how to just be.

We ate a cold lunch and did very little to pass the day. Sarah was more vigilant than I had been about staying awake to reschedule her body on Paris time. I hadn't even been on the flight and all I wanted to do was sleep. My body wanted that rest. I was ready for that rest.

So Sarah occupied herself enjoying time with the kids, like a good nanny, and I went to my cool, quiet nanny bedroom to take a nap after a quick e-mail to my mom. She was dying to have as much correspondence as possible while Sarah and I were together in France. I'd already e-mailed her to reassure her that Sarah arrived safely, but I wanted to make sure she got it. A mother never sleeps, of course, and I wanted to make sure her mind was at ease. She had already replied—I should have known. Ever since I'd written her SOS messages from Beaune and one letter from the deepest part of the country, Melay, she'd been worried sick about me. I scanned through her note, smiling at the sweet words of my mother. And there it was—the answer to my future. I had completely forgotten about it after my trip to hell (the country) and the anticipation of heaven (Sarah's arrival/ticket out of here).

> *Dear Rachel,*
>
> *It's nice that our little song bird is singing again (that's you) since you got back to Paris and since Sarah arrived and since it's getting close to time to return to America. Good on ya! AND yesterday you got a letter of acceptance to graduate school. There is a form you have to fill out and return, but I guess it will have to wait till you return. Hopefully, that will work out OK.*
>
> *OK, must get busy.*
>
> *I love you. Love to Sarah too.*

Huh. So I was in. Interesting. I'd been waiting for the confirmation for so long, but I didn't know what to do now that I had it. I should have felt good, of course. My plan had succeeded. I was going to grad school.

Oh, but plans can be so daunting.

And the form—could it really wait? *It had to*, I thought. After all, I was in Paris, working in a very busy, highly time-consuming, demanding job. These admissions people needed to practice some patience. I couldn't handle all their paperwork at once, and especially not from a foreign country! So I dismissed the obligation from my mind and decided it was a much better thing to go spend quality time with the kids like my good sister Sarah was doing. There was no time for naps in this job, what was I thinking? The kids were, after all, the purpose of my being there.

I left the computer on, left the e-mail open, just sort of staring into the open space of the nanny room, and I climbed up the stairs to join the fun.

We would go to all the wonderful touristy places to-morrow. I couldn't wait to take the kids and I told them all about it. When bedtime finally came, I went to sleep dream-ing of Ladurée and shopping in the original Hermès store. 24, rue Faubourg-Saint Honoré. There's a perfume named after it, for crying out loud; we had to go.

Sarah hated shopping. And really, she didn't overflow with excitement at the thought of visiting a tea room. But I did. I hadn't had anyone here all summer with whom to enjoy these things. We would go, I made us go, and the kids would enjoy it as a fine educational experience. Ladurée, and Hermès, for that matter, were hugely historic icons of Paris.

So off we went, two nannies and two kids. Sarah in-sisted if we were going the route of l'Opéra, we would first stop at the Louvre. Immediately assuming her role as "good" nanny, she urged the kids to bring their sketchbooks so that they could practice their own versions of the masterpieces in-side. I feigned interest, but I was far too concerned with French pastry and this fabulous place called Ladurée. I'd also worn three-inch, open-toed heels and was not breezing along down the Champs as easily as everyone else. I made it all the way to the Jardin des Tuileries before I could not stand any-

Rachel Spencer

more dirt in my shoes. I asked Sarah to give me a piggy-back ride, but she just laughed. I think she thought I was kidding.

By that time it was 1 p.m., and I was willing to bet I wasn't the only one with aching feet and growling stomach. I suggested oh-so-sweetly to Sarah that perhaps we should skip the Louvre and go straight to Ladurée. After all, as a thoughtful, compassionate nanny, I didn't want the kids to go hungry. Sarah smirked. She saw right through me, though she indulged me anyway, the way she has been giving in to my persuasion all our lives together. Such is the nature of sisters.

So we left the Jardin des Tuileries and walked the length of rue Royale from the Place de la Concorde, I with my shortcomings, Sarah with hers, and both of us with a kid on our backs. We talked and laughed our way to the ever-posh and poshly priced heartbeat of *déjeuner à Paris*. *"Macarons!"* Constantin yelled. We walked inside to a parlor colored in romantic hues of pistachio and gold. The setting made the atmosphere decadent.

Ladurée was the *salon du thé* credited with making famous *les macarons*. Personally, I didn't care for macaroons, but fortunately Ladurée has made famous many other sumptuous delights since the house was founded in 1862. Though there were four locations in Paris, it didn't occur to me to visit any besides the original, at 16, rue Royale.

"Bonjour, madame," the hostess said.

"Bonjour!" Constantin said.

"Quatre?" she said.

"Bon!" I said.

Oui would have been a better reply, but I had accepted by now that correct French evaded me when my emotions were in any way heightened. I glided along behind the hostess as she led us up the stairs to our table. I felt a sharp tug on the back of my skirt. Sarah. What had I already done wrong?

"She's seating us for lunch, Rachel," Sarah said.

"I know! Aren't you excited?" I said.

"Umm, it's expensive. I thought we were just having tea and a pastry," Sarah said.

"Oh," I said. "Oops."

It was easy for me to forget I was essentially unemployed and did not have a Donald Trump–size checking account. Sarah was only doing her big-sisterly duty and trying to keep me grounded, but I wasn't going to let her steal my fun. Today we were at Laduree and I'd hardly spent any money since coming to Paris. I was determined to feel like a *comtesse* whether or not Sarah wanted to play along.

The waiter met us at out table. He had a striking face and a charming, elegant manner. And even though he was probably trained to be so, I batted my eyes at him as he delivered the menus, colored in trademark pistachio green with gold filigree. When he walked away, I sighed, looked around me, and smiled. This was the good life. Then I opened the menu and, with one glance at the double-digit numbers next to the entrees, my fantasies of being la comtesse Spencer abruptly departed, and I was just Rachel again. Sarah stared at me from across the table. I hated how she was always right about these things.

"Well," I whispered to Sarah. "Is it too late to just ask for tea and pastries?"

She shot me a look that said "yes" without question. "Rachel, don't even think about it," she said. "That would be totally inappropriate." Truthfully, if I'd been there alone, I wouldn't have thought twice about it. But I'm always surprised at what embarrasses my sister. I swallowed the thought of reserving my cash, and reinvented the *comtesse* inside me. And what a fair. I never knew one could take a *religieuse* in any form besides pastry, but indeed I ordered one with tomates, fromage, and basil. I actually discovered that day that the *religieuse*, made of two squatty balls of dough, was inspired by fat nuns. If there were another country that used food to make a mockery of its own national religion, I hadn't yet visited there. Sarah and the kids both took sandwiches of the most elegant style, one named after Les Champs-Élysées. We talked and laughed and had a ball in the elegant atmosphere. At the other tables, business lunch goers drifted in and out. Mothers and daughters of all ages sat lingering over their own royal gourmet.

Though I am nothing but an ordinary person, little pleases me more than fine dining. If I could afford it, I would take at least one six-course, three-hour meal a week. Back in the day when my credit card said "Rachel S Spencer" but the bills went elsewhere (read: to my parents' house), I was a little more frivolous. My best friend and I would dress up in our favorite black pants and curl our hair for hours before we sped off "downtown" in our dads' cars to whatever Italian restaurant we desired. In those days, I used to regularly judge the quality of a restaurant by the way hot tea was served. If they brought me hot water in a cup with a Lipton tea bag on the saucer, they weren't worth it. If they served hot water in a separate pot and offered me a selection of teas from a charming wooden box, they were clearly a quality establishment, worthy of my continuing patronage. Ladurée understood the importance of such details, hospitality, and astute service, and I was pleased at both the vast selection and presentation of the tea.

On the menu, the teas were listed by flavor with a description of what spices blended to create each unique selection, as though the teas were little entrees themselves. *Charmant.* I ordered the Earl Grey. No one else wanted tea, but I have never had a problem drinking alone. Plus, I couldn't bear the thought of ending our time at Ladurée without tea. I wanted to drink in every ounce from that place—every ounce of Paris. I felt a twinge of sadness knowing few days remained, which drew into an overwhelming sense of remorse the more I thought about it—that I had not lived and breathed every sight and sound of the city every waking moment I had been there. That I had ever complained—about anything, anywhere, anyone— shamed me.

Unaware that Paris didn't last forever for everyone, Léonie and Constantin squirmed in their seats and whined a little, ready to leave. To avoid teary eyes, I resumed the shallow but opulent role of *Comtesse Spencer* and shushed them with a patronizing, sugary sweet smile. Sarah shot me the same eye I'd seen when I'd asked if we should skip lunch and just order pastry.

"You guys want to draw?" Sarah asked the kids. "Here, take your drawing pads and sketch."

I was appalled. She had no qualms with kids sitting in the center of Ladurée, drawing pads and pencils in hand, but I couldn't ask the waiter a simple question. There was a difference in what she expected of me and what she expected of the kids, I supposed. This had never really occurred to me until now.

Not to be outdone, I suggested dessert while I waited for my pot of tea.

"Macarons!" Constantin yelled. "I can take the *macarons!"*

"Of course you can, *bébé*," I said. But the selection was not so simple. Dessert consumed at least five written pages of the menu and the selections ranged from *macarons* to *glaces* to pastries of every taste. There were about twenty-five different flavors of *macarons* at Ladurée. Our handsome waiter stood patiently while Constantin read every one.

"Hmm. I do not know," Constantin said.

So the waiter was kind to suggest a sampling platter for our little sir. When four flavors were chosen, all four of the waiter's suggestions, Constantin was beamingly proud to have completed the task. He was so satisfied that when the waiter reached to take Constantin's menu, Constantin instead reached out and shook the waiter's hand. This, I saw, had become a trademark of Constantin's when in exchange with men of authority. The waiter laughed, but gracefully shook hands and smiled. When the rest of us had stopped laughing, we ordered such delights as *une millefeuille framboise, un éclair café,* and a Ladurée *patisserie traditionelle*: Saint Honoré, which I ordered. It was a prelude to the shops of Faubourg I planned to visit next on my list of things to do with Sarah. The waiter served me a silver pot of hot water, accompanied by a silver canister of sugar cubes, both brown and white. When the waiter poured my Earl Grey it was the perfect color and the perfect temperature. I had to request *du lait*, but I didn't mark it against him. Milk with tea was, after all, British.

Everything was perfect, served either on their charming Limoges or tiny silver platters. We stayed for almost three hours, which was fine with the kids, who kept occupied by scribbling in their sketchbooks. Sure, they didn't have the Mona Lisa in front of them, but there were plenty of lessons to be learned in the culture of Ladurée. Sarah and I relished every one.

I had used most of my good graces with Sarah and the kids by the time we reached rue Faubourg-Saint Honoré. But I didn't mind if we shortened the trip. I was tired too and I didn't want the elegance of our day of dining cheapened by retail greed. Chanel, Dior, Yves Saint Laurent, Hermès lay one right after another. We walked slowly, passing shops and peering in windows until we all agreed it was time to go home.

The next day the good nanny decided *Le Louvre* was not an experience she wanted to miss with the kids. She also insisted

Rachel Spencer

on taking the kids to see *Charlie and the Chocolate Factory*. I wanted nothing to do with either activity. Why would I see a movie in Paris when I could see *Paris*?

I still hadn't been to Notre Dame, the one tourism spot I honestly cared to see. It was, after all, our last real day in Paris and to be there in any form but nostalgic seemed wrong, and I wanted to wallow in it. Sarah was careful not to carry her emotions on her sleeve but I didn't know life any other way. She said I was selfish for not wanting to spend as much time with the kids as possible. I said I'd regret it if I didn't do this. So we set off separately, our last day before Antibes, our last day before the kids went to camp, our last day in Paris besides the one day between Antibes and our flight back home. My eyes welled with tears as I walked along the streets. I felt guilty to have abandoned my role as au pair and even my role as sister. I *was* selfish. But I was also on a journey—one that required me to walk alone. It seemed appropriate that I was alone for the last time in Paris.

Notre Dame was my favorite icon of Paris. To me, churches far outweighed the beauty of fountains or statues or other monuments. I looked at the ancient church from a distance as I walked the length of the Seine. I imagined the hundreds of bricklayers and glassblowers and blacksmiths who worked so hard to build it. I thought of the years that passed as it was being built, and the rubble and piles of debris that lay in place of the steeples and vast stone walls that is now Notre Dame. Just like I used to think growing up around Houston highways, the townspeople must have thought, "There's always construction here!" (Unfortunately on Houston's end, no gothic cathedral ever sprang up in place of the orange cones and bulldozers.)

I followed the two front towers of Notre Dame until I could see where Île de la Cité juts out into La Seine. As if Notre Dame was not captivating enough, she stood on this island, set apart from every other place in Paris. There was a large plaza out front and a beautiful garden behind. Not wanting to fight the crowds near the church's entrance, I made my way along the outer perimeter, in search of a removed café with a perfect view and a perfect cup of *café crème*. But the Friday crowds were too thick, and the surrounding cafés too expensive and disappointingly full of plastic souvenirs and cheap paraphernalia. Disappointed, I walked my last leg around the cathedral, and stumbled onto a surprise entertainment.

Ahead of me on the congested sidewalk I heard music. There were crowds of people cluttered together, craning their necks to get a better view. It was jazz, but with a bluegrass twang to it. To me, it was a tribute to Texas—a tribute to going home. I broke through the throngs of people to see a few men with tattered, worn clothes and tattered, worn instruments. They had a sax, a string bass, a guitar, maybe a couple of other instruments. I listened as they sang an old, familiar tune in English, my dad's favorite hymn, "Just a Closer Walk with Thee." I grew up Southern Baptist and one of the best things I gained from that denomination (though it is often scorned, and though I often scorned it) was a love of singing old hymns. My dad played the clarinet when he was a little boy and if I remember correctly, he once showed me the sheet music to this hymn he had often played. Maybe I imagined that—maybe we had just opened our home version of the Baptist Hymnal, but I was sure, regardless, he loved this hymn. The harmony was not quite blending, and it seemed like their "country" accents were self-imposed, but there in Paris with Notre Dame to my back, I knew they were singing me home.

I walked away. Their voices lingered down the street, past the cheap souvenir shops, past the overcrowded, overpriced cafes. They sounded now more like fingernails on a chalkboard than harmony, but I smiled. I saw myself at 6 years old, in the pew of Beaver Baptist Church in Pennsylvania. I sang my heart out then and there, with no knowledge of a place called Paris. I saw myself at 15, in the pew of Kingwood First Baptist. I sang my heart out then as well, vowing that one day I'd leave that narrow-minded bubble of suburbia. I walked off Île de la Cité onto the Pont de l'Archevêché and back to the rest of Paris. I sang softly the sweet words to that beloved hymn. *"I'll be satisfied as long . . . as I walk, let me walk close to Thee."*

I saw myself at that moment, 23 years old. I remembered fondly all my years at home, and all my days of the summers past. And I realized then and there, I *was* at home.

Diane came home around 6 o'clock that night. Sarah and I met her outside the house. Diane walked up the sidewalk, tanned and more beautiful than ever. She looked slightly different, the way everyone looks different after vacation. Newer, somehow, with a different style, different clothes, happier eyes, and an air of relief upon making it back home. But Sarah knew Diane as the eleven-year-old girl that Léonie was to me, and I could tell that even though Diane had grown, Sarah still saw her that way. I was glad—it eased my mind. Seeing Diane like that with Sarah, I felt like all that had gone wrong between us was washed away. Sarah had experienced what I'd always suspected. Diane was just a little girl.

Sarah ran to meet her and Diane stretched out her arms and cooed noises of "ooh" and "ahh." I stood stunned at how open, cordial, warm, and effortless their embrace and greeting were. I hadn't hugged Diane since our first greeting six weeks before. In what I hoped was a warm gesture, I put my arm around her and patted her back a little to join in the reunion. Diane patted back. This was fine. We could be fine after all. And Sarah was here to make sure everything ended well. We walked inside, we three, arm in arm. Diane radiated the warm, fresh sun of summertime and new adventures. Sarah boasted all the while that Diane was the most beautiful girl in the world—and the coolest. "Are you sure you're just fourteen?" she said.

We ate dinner together as a family—Alex, Estelle, Diane, Léonie, Constantin, together with Sarah and me. The meal was short, effortless, less fuss and production than usual. It was Friday night. We were all tired with early, busy mornings dawning soon.

Chapitre Douze

When I arrived in Paris, I spent the first three weeks questioning whether I really belonged in a city. Growing up, I never considered Houston like a typical city because it was so spread out. Granted, in population it was the United States' fourth largest city after New York, L.A., and Chicago, but there was no walking, no stacks of townhouses piled together, no taxi-ing to and from shops and restaurants like in so many cities. I once lived less than a quarter of a mile from the Galleria, but could get there only by a fifteen-minute car ride dodging highways and mass concrete construction. Aside from a few visits to Chicago, Paris was my first attempt to try out true city life.

But after three weeks, I couldn't get past how dirty, loud and crowded it was. Just before leaving Paris for Beaune I wrote in my journal, "The city is nice, but I think I'm more of a country girl." Yes, I once thought that true. Beaune, as I was calling "country" then, seemed the perfect fit for me. It was big enough to hold a fantastic Saturday market, but small enough to have streets paved with brick that were only intended for walking. There was a feeling of home there for which I was looking and longing. But after a few days of actually being there, and a few more days in the *real* country, I realized that I'd never felt more out of place. Going home to Paris was heaven—I loved it more than ever before. I accepted it for what it was. I craved that city feel. Yet even as fabulous a place as it was, I wasn't convinced I'd found my bit of France there either.

When I was in college, even in high school, I dreamed of studying abroad *en Provence*. But like Paris, Beaune, the Burgundy countryside, and the *real* French country, I worried upon leaving Paris for Antibes that I had romanticized Provence like I had everywhere else. It could have easily been one more situation in which I forced myself to belong just because I believed I should love France. I should speak French and I should love Paris, or at least *some* part of France. Right?

But by the time we reached Antibes, I had my doubts I'd ever find my bit of France. Sarah and I walked out of the train station and I panicked. There was no instant infatuation, or love at first sight. I saw some pretty flowers in a nearby garden, but that was it. So I held my breath as we walked to our rented apartment, waiting for the feeling of *this is it!* to overtake me. I would not lose hope. We dropped off our luggage and followed the street signs to the vielle ville, and I scanned the view. Past the dingy 1970s flats and run-down supermarkets, the sky made a debut from the buildings that clouded it before, and I saw a horizon of azure blue spreading out in the distance before us. And when I realized the street on which we walked ended because the Mediterranean Sea was on the other side, I gasped. I grabbed Sarah's arm and I squealed.

This truly was the place—at last—that would forever be "my bit of France."

After less than one day in Antibes, I loved it, plain and simple. It was one of the many perfect towns in the Côte d'Azur *departement* of the gorgeous region of Provence. We stood before the great sea so bold and beautiful, so serene yet daring—a brilliant blue mass of water. The air was warm and moist with salt, and we stood on the orange earth, composed of gravel and stone and packed clay dirt, and breathed it in. We followed the white, brick stone wall that bordered the sea to the cluster of orange and white stone that was called the "old town." The air smelled rich with soothing salts and ancient sun-baked brick. I looked down at the rocks and wondered for how many centuries they had bathed in the deep blue waters. The smells changed from sun and salt and stone to herbs and olive and tomato, and I knew the market was near.

Sarah, who of course had done her homework and refreshed her memory of the town's highlights, told me that Antibes was famous for the market that, from June to August, was open every morning from 6 a.m. to 1 p.m. We neared the covered plaza cluttered with stalls of fruits, vegetables, meats, cheeses, herbs, artisan's crafts, even clothes. It was a marketplace like no other. Sarah and I vowed to eat as cheaply and freshly as possible while in Antibes so we could blow our money in Paris that last day before flying home. So we set a daily budget of a maximum 5 euros each, which, upon smelling one of the famous Provencal pizzas baking in the cafes that lined the streets, I promptly decided we would start the *next* day. At the moment, I had to splurge.

Diving right into the spirit of the Mediterranean, I ordered a pizza Napolitaine. I was aware that the pizza, native to Napoli, Italy, consisted of tomato, basil, cheese, and anchovy, and I even expanded the flavor of the Mediterranean by adding olives. In any other circumstance, I hated anchovies and I rarely ate olives. Sarah, ever the careful one, warned me about the anchovies. *I know*, I said. But it was my first day in Antibes—my new favorite place on Earth—and both anchovies and olives sounded like a fantastic idea. I wanted the real thing. But the anchovies were not the same as the clean, boneless, white filet anchovies Alex had offered me as an appetizer one night back in Paris. They looked like the stuff Garfield the Cat ate in that cartoon, and they smelled like the stuff we fed our cats at my mom's house. They were long, limp, and hairy. But I had ordered them, and since I was still out of my mind in love with Antibes and everything about the Mediterranean, I cut a huge bite and stuffed it in my mouth.

The pizza tasted as bad as it smelled. And the olives I paid extra for were whole with huge, hard seeds that nearly broke my teeth. Sarah had stopped eating at this point. She sat back in her chair with arms crossed, watching me chew. She was laughing so hard at my facial expression that she was nearly crying. I knew she was waiting for me to admit I was wrong, but the taste was so bad that I couldn't speak or I would have gladly surrendered. Despite her laughter at my expense, Sarah was sweet and sympathetic. She offered me half of her *quatre fromage,* but I had lost my appetite. *Quelle surprise.* It took days before the taste left my mouth and even longer before it left my memory.

Rachel Spencer

The positive thing about eating an anchovy pizza with whole olives within the first hour of arriving in Antibes was that I knew things would only get better from there. Provence, Antibes, and the sea had a week to prove it to me and I knew they all would, hairy anchovies aside. We retreated early to our apartment that night, tired from a day of travel. We watched *Sabrina* in bed on my laptop and cooed that now we had both made over our lives by living in Paris. We dreamed about future visits and fantasized about sporting our fabulous Mediterranean tans back at home.

I woke up earlier than usual the next morning. Something about the Mediterranean sun on the rise hastened me to seize every moment of daylight. I tiptoed out of our tiny rented studio to take a morning walk through town in search of a bakery.

There were no signs for *rétrodors* outside the shops in Antibes. Most of the shops weren't open, actually. August. Everyone left their jobs for the month of *vacances*, perhaps. When I found an open shop with a morning assortment, I shrugged, missing Ruddy Cheeks and knowing just by the looks of things that these pastries couldn't begin to compete with hers. I bought several regardless of that, and regardless of the fact that I was again breaking our 5 euros-a-day budget. But I felt the need to spoil Sarah with a wide selection.

She was awake when I returned home. The tea kettle whistled in the kitchen. She found in our partially stocked cabinets two essentials: instant coffee and salt. I put aside my espresso snob attitude for the morning, knowing I'd rather pour brown grounds into boiling water than go without morning coffee.

We took our pastry breakfast on the patio balcony of our second-floor apartment, which offered not a view of the Mediterranean, but a view of concrete and other flat, 1970s-style buildings. Still, I didn't care. It was our balcony and I loved it. We sipped our instant coffee and took bites from the assortment of pastries and welcomed the morning slowly and peacefully. Even as I ate breakfast, I was planning my next meal.

To me, food is culture. Hairy anchovies and unpitted olives aside, I loved the flavors associated with the Mediterranean. We walked the sea wall to the market that bustled more in the mid-morning than it had upon our late noon arrival the day before. Our eyes widened at the rows of fresh produce, flowers, meats, cheeses, and spices. It smelled like morning—a Provencal morning with loads of goods fresh from the farmers' trucks. Locals and tourists strolled from counter to counter dressed in T-shirts and beach cover-ups. They barely covered their tanned feet with sandals. Many of them had tattoos. They were rough but friendly, slouchy but cool. Behind the stalls, the sellers and farmers possessed a glow to their skin, kissed by the orange and yellow Mediterranean sun.

I developed an apricot obsession during my time in France. It was my saving grace and I smuggled them into my room on the worst days, and ate them alone. They were just

Rachel Spencer

so tiny and cute to start, but also the most deliciously tart and juicy fruit I'd ever popped in my mouth. My goal at the market was to find the cheapest and the best *abricots* for sale and buy a bundle. It was imperative I began strict adherance to our budget. We searched the stalls for the cheapest ones and found some at 2.50 euros per kilo.

"*Bonjour, mademoiselles!*" a skinny, leather-skinned Provencal man at the produce stand said. "*Un goûter, non?*" he said.

"*Merci, monsieur,*" we said in unison.

"*Un photo?*" he said.

"Oh good!" Sarah said to me. "Someone to take our picture!" She handed him the camera, saying thank you.

"*Non, non,*" the friendly Provencal man said. "*Moi, moi.*" He handed the camera back. Sarah and I looked at each other and laughed while the Provencal man struck a pose over his golden orange display of *abricots*. We snapped the shot, still laughing. He clapped and said, "Bravo!" with a French accent. From his *abricots* display, Sarah and I bought *une livre,* or half a kilo, for 1.25.

"*Attendez, attendez,*" the skinny Provencal man said. We turned, smiling, as he handed us each a freshly cut slice of cantaloupe. I let the sticky warm juices run down my chin while I laughed in sheer delight.

Taste-testing our way from one stall to the next, we bought two plump, red tomatoes. At the other end, the lettuce was cheap and robust in variety, so we bought some mesclun and roquette for less than one euro total. We were certain we couldn't eat sun-fed juicy tomatoes without basil.

So Sarah asked the lettuce lady if she sold any basil by the leaf or branch, aside from the potted plant variety at her stand. (It was priced at a daring 2.50 euros and that would have eaten one-fourth of our total daily budget.) The lady showed us the thick, tied bundles she sold but that, too, was too much for two people and two tomatoes. She got the hint—we were only interested in a handful of leaves *pour les tomates.*

"*Un petit peu?*" she asked.

"*Oui, trop petit,*" I replied. She took a few stems from her tied bundle and handed them to me.

"*Combien?*" I asked, expecting her to say maybe 50 centimes.

"Non, non," she said. She shook her head back and forth—no cost, no. She smiled at us.

We definitely weren't in Paris anymore.

Walking out of the market, we passed a stall full of chèvre. I hope I never learn to resist chèvre and I certainly didn't try to that day. One round of *chèvre frais* for 2.30 euros and our daily trip was complete for under 6 euros. Four more remained between our two budgets so we bought two baguettes, one for lunch and one—a little prematurely—for dinner.

At last we ventured beyond the sea wall to the cool shore of the Mediterranean. Time to start baking ourselves and gobbling our market fare. We soaked in the full sun as we ripped into our plastic sacs, brown paper bags, wax paper, and little pieces of tissue. Our lunch was simple but delicious as everything is when eaten with a beach appetite. I sat on my towel in the sand and ate one apricot after another on a slice of baguette smeared with the deliciously fresh goat cheese. Sarah ate the same and we saved some apricots and bread for later in the afternoon when we knew a few hours in the sun would re-create an appetite.

Hours later after sweat, sand, and sea, we were back in town. I was sun-soaked, relaxed, and happier than I'd been in a long time. The trip was definitely the ultimate reward for my hard weeks as a nanny, and I was determined to soak up every moment of it before returning to the U.S., where real life and real responsibilities awaited me. I swore to myself before I left the *Chronicle*—actually, I prayed—that I would never again consider an 8-to-5 cubicle-enclosed, desk job. I knew by now I wanted more than that, but I also knew I was putting off real life. Nannying was sort of a holding period. It wasn't my life I was living, it was somebody else's, though I felt at ease enjoying such a luxurious lack of responsibility. But my days were numbered. Soon I would have bills to pay and decisions to make and responsibilities to carry out. I hated the thought of surrendering to another cubicle to pay those bills. Maybe I could live on student loans and prolong real life for another couple of semesters—debt seemed to be a popular way of life among people my age, anyway. But money and jobs were not issues that should plague anyone's mind under the full sun of the Mediterranean. So I ignored the future as best I could, and soaked in more of the golden delicious rays of the present.

Channeling Alex, I bought olive oil and vinegar (dipping into the souvenir budget) for dinner preparation that night. Once home and refreshed after a dirty day outdoors, I sliced up the tomatoes, exposing their velvety red insides. I bathed them in a marinade of balsamic vinegar, olive oil, salt, and fresh basil while I tossed the mesclun and roquette in more of the same sauce.

The baguette did not cut as smoothly as the tomatoes, as it was half a day old and I had to saw through it with a tiny butter knife. So I gripped it with one hand and began gently sawing at an angle. It wouldn't budge. So I sawed harder and the chewy bread gave way a bit. Encouraged, I sawed harder and harder and had one round cut! Victorious! From there, I proceeded with ease, befriending the knife and thinking that Alex would be so proud of my ability to make do with such primitive tools. I cut several more pieces and had gained a good rhythm when I got careless. One minute, I was happily sawing through the bread, the next I was seized with numbing, near-blackout pain. I must have shrieked because I faintly remembered Sarah yelling, "What?!" in sheer panic. Somehow I made it to the balcony patio outside in hopes that the fresh air would erase the incident or at least keep me from blacking out.

"Rachel, your eyes are rolling back in your head," Sarah said, sounding panicked.

I didn't speak, couldn't speak. And I didn't open my eyes, either. I was terrified of seeing my own blood.

"Rachel, do I need to take you to the emergency room?"

"No!" I yelled.

"Well, I need you to get up," Sarah said.

"No!" I yelled.

Rachel Spencer

"Rachel . . ."

"No!" I yelled.

"Okay, okay. Just stay there." Sarah came back onto the balcony with a wet dishtowel and wrapped my cut and bloodied finger while I whimpered in pain. I swore I'd cut a bone or something and I dared not look to see. In the bloodied wet towel, I held my hand over my head while Sarah looked on with a pained expression.

Like Paris, there wasn't a pharmacy or any store open past five o'clock, so Sarah wrapped a tight tourniquet of toilet paper around the sliced finger and tied it off with dental floss. It wasn't perfect, but it would do. Once the pain and panic subsided a bit, my optimistic spirit took over. I was determined to create the perfect French beach vacation dinner, and I wasn't letting a stupid bloody finger stop me! I inched my way up toward standing again and, holding my hand above my head, returned to the kitchen. I kept my hand in the air, and Sarah indulged my stubbornness, holding down the loaf while I sliced the remaining portion into rounds. Together we fried them in oil on the stovetop. Just before browning, we added *crottins* of chèvre to the tops of the bread rounds, allowing them to melt only slightly. We served them warm over our bed of salad and ate the marinated tomatoes alongside. The meal was a little primitive, but well earned and naturally delicious! With such fresh produce, little needs to be added. And after trauma, anything tastes good.

We completed our first full day on budget and had apricots to spare for dessert. It wasn't a meal of Alex-size proportions, but it was simple, fresh, and satisfying—and I had done it myself. As I crawled into bed that night, sleepy, happy, and with my bandaged finger, I realized something. Six weeks ago, in this same situation, I would have given up and gone to bed without dinner. But now here I was, more confident, more calm (sort of) and more willing to take charge of the world around me. It was a small progression, but a good one. Before I drifted off to sleep that night, I promised myself that my newfound courage would not end with France. I would take it back across the Atlantic Ocean and to whatever new experiences awaited me. As for my finger—in the morning, I would experience a very local side of Antibes at the pharmacy, if I could find one.

Did going to the doctor christen me as a local? If so, I would have transferred citizenship right then and there. Well, for a short time, perhaps. Nevertheless, I felt like a French citizen, seeking out the benefits of free medical care at last. Like everything else in France, local pharmacies had not been bought out by conglomerates and mega stores. You could spot them by the bright green neon crosses in their windows. It had always seemed so quaint to me. That is, until I incurred a minor injury and needed care on a Sunday. Then the quaintness quickly turned to frustration—the pharmacy would not re-open until 2:30 p.m. the next day. I had flashbacks to *l'opticien*, but Sarah and I made the best of it, and spent the day lazing in the sun.

I woke up early Monday before Sarah and set off in search of a breakfast treat. I'd just come out of a bakery with a bag of fresh croissants when I noted a green cross lit on the building a couple doors down. Could it be? A pharmacist who broke the closed-Mondays rule of French business? The door was open and a kind, white-coated pharmacist welcomed me inside. *C'est vrai!* He took one look at my makeshift attempt at health care and motioned me back to his workspace. He pulled out a doctor's kit full of all kinds of gadgets and packages.

He removed the toilet paper and we both winced a little at the nasty sight of my rather deep cut gone unattended for twelve hours. Of course I had no idea how to tell him what I needed, so I resorted to Franglais. *Antiseptique* didn't seem to translate that well to him, but he did squeeze a few drops of something medicinal-smelling onto the cut. Hoping for some Neosporin, I asked, *"Crème d'antibiotique?"* I wasn't sure if I was making any sense, but he spread a greenish-yellow ointment into the cut. He taped, gauzed, and wrapped my finger so I looked like a regular war hero—a kitchen war hero.

Like so many of the Frenchmen I'd met on my trip, he had quite a sense of humor. On cutting the excess tape, he pretended he took scissors to my finger—the injured one—and made silly attack noises while he clipped the scissors in the air. This did little to comfort me, as I'd spent the previous night trying to get the image of the knife slipping from the baguette and into my finger out of my mind. But, despite the cruel humor, he had made it all better. And to confirm the rumor I'd heard and wanted to believe about French government and medical services, he charged me nothing. It was almost worth the cut just to get personal medical attention free of charge.

Sarah and I spent the day mostly in the sun, taking special care to stay away from knives (and chewy, stale baguettes). Sarah washed my hair for me that night as I really couldn't do it alone with just one hand. She took good care of me, and we watched *Sabrina* in bed again, just for comfort's sake. The day that followed blended together hours of sun, swim, long walks, and fresh market finds. We ate and tanned mostly, walking only to dry off the excess water from a swim before we dove in again. The beaches were crowded, many in the topless fashion of Anne-Laure. I tried to adjust, though I knew I would never be completely comfortable so *au naturel*.

After several days of lazing around, Sarah and I both decided we could not be so close to the Italian border without crossing it. We got a crazy idea. We went to Europcar around 10 a.m. that morning, hoping they would have *un décapotable* available for rent. Sure, renting a convertible was twice the price of the funny-shaped European cars, but if we were going to cruise along the Riviera straight into Italy, we were going to do it in style.

The woman behind the counter said they had a French-made cabriolet available. We weren't sold. Sarah and I looked at each other, making "I don't know" faces. Maybe we would try the Hertz rental place by the train station. But then, out of the jumble of French words, I heard something familiar—Volkswagen.

I have to admit, I've always been charmed by Volkswagens, thanks to their genius marketing efforts. They drew me in with the ad where teenage, maybe college-aged kids drove the convertible at night, listened to good music, and looked at the stars. The commercials always encompassed both youth and responsibility, and since I was trying so hard to hang on to both, I felt confident that even I could be a driver of a Volkswagen.

We turned to the woman behind the counter and asked, *"Le Volkswagen—C'est la même prix que le cabriolet?"* Surely a bug convertible wasn't the same price as a boxy French convertible with almost no style?

"Mais, oui," she replied.

Our eyes glimmered. The transaction was made. Freedom was so close I could smell it. Soon I would be zooming along the coast, creating my own Volkswagen commercial as I went along. But alas, I am not the responsible sister. A responsible sister would have remembered to bring her driver's license. And the responsible sister did. So I let Sarah take the wheel.

Minutes later, we met Bugsy. She came smiling around the corner, a beautiful cream-colored car with black convertible top. She was the perfect Riviera ride. Bugsy was a faithful friend—the type who gave cheerfully, not expecting anything in return. I wished I had a flower to put in her vase inside, but I knew she didn't mind too much to leave it empty. Bugsy was the happy-natured type who just wanted everyone to have a good time. The more the merrier—that was Bugsy's motto.

We hopped in, and zoomed off toward the *bord de mer*, like Bugsy was made to drive no other route. We introduced her to Chris Martin and his folks and went flying to the song, "Fix You," that I believed would land Coldplay a permanent place in the Rock and Roll Hall of Fame right next to U2.

There was no better song to hear at that moment, on that day. We listened to it on repeat from Antibes to Italy and back. It was a song about getting what you want, but not what you need. It was all about failing but going on anyway. Loving, knowing that losing love is the worst thing in the world—the most, awful, painful, God-forsaken thing in the world that still doesn't kill you—but letting go of love all the same. And after all is said and done, ruined and wasted, dead and irreparable, there is life again. Life from death. Beauty from ashes. A new thing happening even in the dead of winter. Branches crack. The ground is frozen. And it's only by your breath coming out in frosted puffs that you know you're still breathing. But then from nothing, something. You wake up one day and it is the hottest summer of your life. And you see that after all that cold, dark gray of winter, you're sweating so much you can hardly stand it.

We sped along the *bord de mer*. I blasted the volume as high as it could go. Sarah winced a little, but she let me do it anyway. It was a thrill—a boiling hot thrill. It was the greatest time of my life.

Tears streamed down my face. I let go of all the things I thought had been lost. I once thought I lost everything I knew, and I had given up to become someone I never wanted to be.

Rachel Spencer

And I never wanted to go back again.

But there was more. There was redemption. This is what happens when you trust—when you jump out in faith. When you forgive. When everything hurts like hell, but you learn how to say, "I messed up." So what. You move on. You say after that, "Oh well." There's more to come if you want. There's life after death. There's hope—and with the wind hitting my face faster than it ever had, with the amazing bright blue of the Mediterranean sea stretching to my right as far as I could see, the bright orange ball of sun radiating, bouncing light off the waves onto my skin, there was even *fun*. Fun! And there was home.

Home was coming. If I could face it, if I could learn from it, if I could just live and be, I would go home soon.

Chapitre Treize

So we went home. Home to Paris, that is, for one more day and two more nights before going home for good to the States. Sarah and I passed the second to last evening quietly. We ate dinner at my favorite pizza place near the Vladescos' house. San Remo, it was called. And now that I had driven through Italy and to the town of San Remo before we turned Bugsy around, it seemed the most appropriate place to conclude our trip. Plus, I was desperate to redeem that horrible anchovy episode in Antibes.

I ordered pizza with garlic, gorgonzola, and tomato. Sarah had four-cheese, and we split a *salade césar* and a bottle of red wine. A great homecoming meal back in that city of lights and love. But everything felt, even tasted, bittersweet. Tomorrow was the last day. Then the journey would be over and I would have to start living out whatever it was I had learned. But the journey was never truly over.

So much was left unwritten, so much was left undone. But I knew that was the point of places like Paris. You can't ever see or do it all so you keep craving it. You keep coming back. You keep believing it's the greatest place on Earth because you're not really sure yet what kind of place it is.

In true American tourist form, I spent our last day blowing money and time on frivolous things as planned, dragging Sarah along with me. Chocolate, wine, gift boxes of macaroons from Ladurée, all things that perish, all things that must be enjoyed in a moment, then committed to memory. Just like Paris. We came home for our last dinner on the garden patio, *chez Vladesco*, the best restaurant in town.

The air was warm and sweet. Softer, quieter, slower than the first day I arrived. All the lanterns were lit in the garden, casting a golden glow on the table. Wanting to keep the moment in my mind, I walked out and sat at the table alone. Alex stood boastfully over the grill, humming and muttering to himself in his usual grand chef way. He kissed his fingers and looked back at me, grinning in delight at his work of perfection. Knowingly, I smiled back.

That night, we feasted on langoustine, which sounds twice as elegant and palatable as feasting on "large prawns," as we'd say it in English. Alex had ordered from the *poissonerie* especially for our last supper together. He had them delivered fresh from both the coasts of Brittany and Scotland because, *bien sûr*, the best langoustines come from the coasts of Brittany and Scotland. Far be it for me to relay to the grand chef my intense disgust for shellfish of any origin. Still, I was flattered by the obvious gesture the meal implied and tried convincing myself that my last night in Paris would be the night I fell in love with shellfish. Or maybe not. Maybe I would eat it and hate it but eat it anyway because I'd fallen in love with the Vladescos and with Paris and with their house and with everything in the past six weeks of my life.

Estelle stood halfway out the sliding glass door, sucking on a cigarette. She stared off, unaffected by her fussing husband. She was always staring off, but I understood now as I hadn't before that her silence was not so much a lack of interest as it was a quiet appreciation of the company of others.

I walked inside to see what mischief Léonie and Constantin were concocting and ran into Constantin on his way out. He ran straight to Estelle, and Estelle, not looking down, brushed her hand over his tiny head. He tugged at her until she looked to see the picture he had just drawn for her. *"Je t'aime, Maman,"* the picture read in words drawn with black marker over a colored red heart. She cooed a little, reveling in the brilliance and sweetness of her youngest child. He was satisfied with her loving attention, little Alex that he is, and, handing her the picture, he turned to run off again, and I followed my 7-year-old dictator inside. He turned to be certain I was following him, as it is very important that he receive attention at all times, but once he saw I was in fact exactly where he wanted me, he lost interest. It is his cool, aloof way of loving those around him.

When I first arrived under the domination of Monsieur Constantin, this sort of behavior both infuriated and intimidated me. I was sure there was no way to love or attend to such a demanding child. Now I knew his looking back at me meant he needed me and in fact, wanted me, even though he pretended he did not. I was happy to do it for the short and rare and precious time we had left.

He ran to the bottom of the stairs where he cried, *"Léoniiiiiieeee!!! À table!"*

Léonie of course was upstairs instant messaging back and forth to her friends. She almost never replied to the first call to dinner, and Constantin never stopped yelling until he received a reply. Before he could rattle the windows again I scooped him up and swung him around. He screamed and cried and giggled deliriously as he was prone to do. I put him down, and said up the stairs loudly but gently, "Léonie, come down." Then I grabbled his little hand and led him to the patio for dinner. There was a time when I would have stood at the bottom of the stairs, waiting for Léonie, but now I knew she would come down when she was ready. And she was always ready pretty close to the time she needed to be.

Diane, who had been dozing in her room, was late to dinner. As if to illustrate just how much things had changed, when we all took our places at the table, Diane slid into the seat next to me and confided that she'd stayed out until five o'clock in the morning. She'd done the same thing her last night in Spain, she'd told me. What did a fourteen-year-old girl do in the streets of Seville until five o'clock in the morning with complete strangers? I remembered staying up that late with friends when I was fourteen in my parents' house. I thought that was a big deal. Diane, on the other hand, thought nothing of partying through the wee morning hours. But looking at her, I thought she might be glad to be home. I raised my eyebrows in response to her confession, laughed a little with her, and put my arm around her to hug her. It was a gesture that I think reassured me more than it did her, but regardless, here we all were together for the last supper. There were expressions of soft contentment on everyone's faces.

I looked around the table and felt as though I was looking at where I had come from and where I was now and where I was going—even if I didn't know where that was yet. But I knew this ending had to be the beginning of something good. Maybe a master's in journalism wasn't the ticket to something good. Maybe it didn't matter if I never filled out the forms, if I missed registration. I didn't have to know the right decision right away. It wasn't about whether I turned to the right, or whether I turned to the left, it was just about whether I kept walking. I just had to keep going. It wasn't the end, but the road.

"Bon!" Alex grunted satisfyingly, commencing the meal with his word of choice. Without delay, he grabbed for his show of langoustine, buttered and broiled, and placed one, two, three, four langoustines on his plate.

"They're very small, you know? So you have to take several," Alex informed us, justifying the mounting excitement on his face as his pile grew taller and taller. "Just crack them open and pull the meat. There's not much meat on them so you have to take several," he repeated, as if by way of explanation.

I sat trying not to gag at the thought of actually cracking the shell of a once-living creature when Constantin, who had already begun the process, started wailing.

"Constantin, *qu'est-ce qui se passé?*" Alex said. Constantin, still crying, said nothing and pointed to his plate that, aside from one langoustine, was filled with a puddle of bluish black ink. Again trying not to gag, I consoled Constantin, who was sitting to my left, as best I could. I wanted to say, "Yeah, aren't they disgusting?" But of course I didn't.

"Hand me the plate," Alex demanded. I did, and watched him wipe it clean with a slice of baguette before he handed it back to me.

"It's good, Constantin?" his father said, gesturing to the now clean plate. But Constantin would not be swayed. Much like his father might, he refused to eat on a plate that had been sprayed with the foulness of a bad langoustine.

"Hmph." Constantin folded his arms across his chest in insolence and sat staring putridly at the plate before him until Estelle instructed Léonie to get him a clean plate. Indeed, he was the *petit monsieur* of the house.

With Constantin satisfied, I had to face my own plate of scary langoustines. They stared back at me with little ball-shaped black eyes, daring me to try them. I hesitated to touch them in fear of a second inking episode. "Okay, Alex," I said. "I need some instruction on how to eat these!"

"You just rip the head from the body and pull the meat out," Alex replied, as if everyone in the world knew how to eat langoustines except for me.

Stalling for time, I was about to ask him to approve my shell-cracking method when, sensing my hesitation, he stopped me before I could bother him with another question and said, "Oh, just shut up and eat it!"

He laughed. Everyone laughed. And I'd learned that Alex meant no harm, so I laughed too. It was impossible to be offended in the pleasure of such fine food and company. There were no offenses here. Especially not at the table. So I shut up and ate the langoustine, cracking the shell, avoiding the ink, and pulling out the silky white flesh of meat inside.

My plate was full. In addition to the langoustines, there was green salad with vinaigrette that I'd prepared, as had become the dinnertime ritual. It would be ridiculous to say that, after about five weeks of practice, I had perfected the art of making homemade vinaigrette. Nevertheless, week after week, Alex trusted me to whip together some Dijon with vinegar, oil, salt, pepper, and whatever else inspired me to taste. For the final meal, I made the sauce with some added lemon juice and a little white wine.

"Pas mal," he commended me when he tasted it. "No, in fact. It's good. Very good!" So I sat and ate my own salad, enjoying the taste more so than usual knowing the grand chef approved.

Course by course, we ate our last supper together, and afterwards, we toasted with a glass of champagne. Actually it was several glasses of champagne, but doesn't champagne have a bubbly way of causing us to ignore the silly details?

Once all the food had been eaten and the wine drunk, I stumbled up from my seat to present Estelle and Alex with a small gift. I offered a velvety brown box from Maison du Chocolat full of champagne truffles. Never mind the Vladescos would never overdose on a box of decadent choco-late, but it was luxury nonetheless, and during my time with them, they had taught me that the art of luxury is not about size, it's about enjoyment of something fine and simple. What on earth else could I possibly offer this family? Estelle also had a gift for me, and for Sarah. She presented us with a fragrance from a store whose name I didn't recognize. But Diane wanted it, which meant it was probably very nice or very cool, and probably both.

I kissed the girls and Constantin one by one as they flitted from the table off to bed. Well, Léonie and Constantin flitted; Diane moved slowly, probably from the combination of too much champagne and too little sleep. So I walked her to her room and bid her good-bye, and behind her eyes was the look of a little girl who might need a nanny more than either of us realized.

Then I looked into Léonie and Constantin's rooms. Léonie looked up at me from her bed, where she was sitting and reading a book. She regarded me for a moment, then turned her attention back to her reading. I stood there, feeling her quiet, passionate intensity. She was so special. I wanted to be there when all she had been storing inside her spilled over into greatness. I knew it would—she was bound for greatness.

Then in rapid movement, Léonie leapt from her bed and ran to me. She refused to look up but kept her head pressed into my leg while she wailed. She really wailed. She cried and begged me not to leave, like if I did I would be betraying her. I didn't want to leave. Sure, there was a life waiting for me somewhere else, and it was time to go live that life

I'd thought about so much. But little Léonie the Star had asked me to stay. And I took it as the highest compliment.

I was gripping her tiny toned arms and squeezing my eyes shut to avoid tears when I felt short pawlike strokes on my own arms. It was Constantin; he had come to comfort us. He stood at our side, petting both of us with his sweet little hands. His eyes were closed. His lashes rested still against his pink cheeks, and a smile spread across his contented face. I kissed the babies good-bye. I would be back, I told them, as I fought back my own tears. I had to come back. There would always be a reason for me here. Then I climbed slowly down the stairs to the main floor and then down again to the nanny bedroom where Sarah was already sleeping.

In Paris more than any other place, I found it impossible to sleep. And when I climbed into bed that night, Ella Fitzgerald singing "At Duke's Place" drifted down the stairs and into my basement bedroom. I couldn't see him, but I knew that Alex sat in his living room, listening to music, puffing a cigar and tapping his feet. I wondered how he maintained a lifestyle of late nights and 10- or 12-hour work days, but this balance of work and pleasure, where pleasure seemed to outweigh every possible burden, was one of many mysteries of Paris, of *les Vladesco*, of Alex and Estelle, that was too wonderful to question. And I realized that I didn't have to question it anymore. So I just accepted it and listened to his music from my room.

It was 2 a.m. and I lay wide awake, counting the days

and hours since my plane left for Paris. I lay there making mental lists of all that I hadn't done, all that was yet to be done in this city. I thought of the days waiting for me back in Houston. I thought of wherever it was I was going in Arkansas. I thought of all the days waiting for me in the years to come— all of the days when I would look back and remember this very moment and long for the freedom, the peace, the love I found in Paris.

I could have walked the streets of Paris all day, every day, from the day I came until my plane took off again. Even then, I wouldn't have walked enough.

What was it about being in Paris that made the filth and grime endearing? Dirty streets, stinky rubbish, graffiti-covered concrete walls; oh, I loved the horrible, wonderful sight of it all. This life was full of agony and ecstasy. One contradiction after another had kept me thirsty for years. I yearned to be a part—to be hurled into the great black hole of middle that was the mess of life. Perhaps I was there. I couldn't tell. I only knew I was thirstier than ever. Maybe that was the key—not the knowing, just the thirst. And the thirst gave way to knowing. I knew what to expect—expect anything, actually. And expect everything.

Anything less was just not Paris. Anything less was just not me.

I listened to the night air waft in and out of my nanny room windows, as I lay there, stiff and still. I knew morning would come too soon. Morning always came too soon when clocks were ticking. And clocks that I hadn't heard since I left home were ticking—even if only in my mind. But I would just take my café a little stronger the next day. And then, the sunrise.

As I lay there, I remembered something I read from one of Alex's cookbooks by an English chef. One of the chef's new hires complained about being tired after only six hours of sleep. The chef looked at him disgustedly and said, "If you sleep six hours every night you'll have slept for fifteen years by the time you're sixty. Doesn't that scare [you to death]?" "Yes," the new hire said. "Then go home and sleep four hours, and when you're sixty, you'll have only wasted ten."

I didn't do the math, but the concept seemed appropriate. I'd slept too much already. So I was content to lie there and listen to the funny sirens and dissonant horns and wait until I smelled baking bread at the *boulangerie* around the corner.

Then I would gather my things, buy one last croissant or maybe two, and get on a plane to go back to where I came from. Home. I guess I'd been going there all along.

ACKNOWLEDGMENTS

I've missed setting the table. I've missed the water decanters and wine bottles at every meal. I've even missed the personalized napkin rings. But when I was there, I missed Southern summers. I missed the Fourth of July. I missed oversized, overpriced lattes. And now of course, I miss and dream of that fantastic espresso machine. But loving both places, loving both lives is all part of it.

To *les Vladesco*, I thank you for offering me that other life for just one brief moment. I owe you all much more than this. Léonie, I had a dream the other night you were a ballerina—you were the best one on stage, *bien sûr*. I love all of you very much—and your family in all corners of the city and country.

To my Svengali, Dwight Silverman, thank you for naming this book, first the blog, then allowing us to carry on the title. Thanks to all dear friends at the *Houston Chronicle*— to Stephen Weis and Jeff Cohen who urged me to pitch the blog at all; to Scott Clark who gave the stamp of approval; to my old team (here's where I write Deanna Marie Jewell

Barrett) and to Kim Michell. I'll always love the *Chronicle*—thank you.

To my editor, Danielle Chiotti, who edited my book alongside planning her wedding, thank you for risking so much with me. Thanks to Kensington Publishing and Danielle alike for offering me the contract and for hours of dedicated, tedious work. Thanks to my agent, William, who advised me both inside and outside publishing. Thank you to my friend Dan Limke who so kindly indulged me for my first ever "photo shoot."

To Nitty, thank you for introducing all of us to *les Vladesco*, and thank you for introducing me to nearly everything. You always take care of me, always indulge me, and then somehow still love me despite my vanity and abrasiveness. I thank all of my family and friends who have supported me through this. "I no have notion of loving people by halves . . . My attachments are always excessively strong."
—Jane Austen, *Northanger Abbey*.

I am most recently indebted to the *Arkansas Democrat-Gazette*. To David Brown and to John Mobbs, thank you for caring about me beyond work. You know I want to make you proud, and despite immense frustration and my sick attitude many days, you know I'm grateful.

I'd also like to thank a few of my first teachers in writing, though there is a lifetime of work ahead of me, and I'll probably remain eternally intimidated by you. I think of all of you often, more than I ever let on. Thank you, Lindy Nelson, Melissa Hayhurst, Dr. Louise Montgomery, Gerald Jordan, and Miller Williams. Some teachers have discouraged me, but you are the reason I want to keep learning.

Above all, thank you, readers. Readers of the blog, you were such an inspiration. And readers of this book—whether you liked it or hated it, thank you for reading. Cheers and *bon courage.*